S. C. Biela

IN THE ARMS
OF MARY

D0169802

COMMUNION OF LIFE WITH CHRIST THROUGH MARY

Orange, CA
Revised Second Edition

Nihil Obstat   +Most Reverend Jaime Soto
                    Auxiliary Bishop
                    Censor
Imprimatur   +Most Reverend Tod D. Brown
                    Bishop of Orange, California
                    USA – May 16, 2002

According to Canon 830, I find the work, In the Arms of Mary to be free from doctrinal and moral error. This is not intended to imply agreement with the content or the opinions expressed.

Revised Second Edition 2005
Copyright © 2002 by Slawomir Biela
First published in Great Britain in February 2002 under the title
Praying Self-Abandonment to Divine Love ISBN 1-85873-941-1

Published by
In the Arms of Mary Foundation
P.O. Box 271987, Fort Collins, CO 80527-1987
E-mail address: inquiry@IntheArmsofMary.org
Website: www.IntheArmsofMary.org

For more information about the Foundation "In the Arms of Mary" or to obtain additional copies of this book, please visit us at our website (see back pages of this book for more details).

Translated by
Very Rev. Jaroslaw Zaniewski

Edited by
Frederick M. Baedeker, Jr.   Michelle L. Curtis   Phyllis M. Crews

Cover and text designed by
Ewa Krepsztul

Cover artwork by
Rosemary Mertz / Our Lady of Guadalupe and St. Juan Diego
Copyright © In the Arms of Mary Foundation

ISBN 0-9721432-9-7 (Softback)
ISBN 0-933314-00-1 (Hardback)

In memory of William Joseph Bartee, Jr.
This printing was made possible by the financial support of his family.
Your prayers are appreciated.

Printed in the United States of America

I have come to set the earth on fire, and
how I wish it were already blazing! (Lk 12:49)

To our beloved Holy Father John Paul II,
who fervently desires that the fire of the
New Evangelization were already blazing.

Contents

FOREWORDS BY

Theodore Cardinal McCarrick
Archbishop of Washington

Norberto Cardinal Rivera Carrera
Archbishop Primate of Mexico

Ricard María Cardinal Carles Gordó
Archbishop of Barcelona

Jaime Cardinal L. Sin
Archbishop of Manila

Stephen Cardinal Kim Sou-hwan
Archbishop Emeritus of Seoul

Theodore Cardinal McCarrick
Archbishop of Washington

I n this third millennium, as we continue to respond to our Holy Father, Pope John Paul II's call to the New Evangelization, we must also remember that we, as individuals, are also being prompted by the spirituality of events in our lives to respond even more eagerly to God's call to sanctity. As the New Evangelization implies, this response calls for a renewed zeal and sincere openness to the Holy Spirit, the kind of openness which allows us to ". . . seek first the kingdom [of God] and his righteousness . . ." (Mt 6:33). Exemplifying such a response to God's call through his own profoundly deep spiritual life, the Holy Father reminds us of Christ's challenge to trust boldly in Him as we "'put out [our] nets into the deep for a catch'" (cf. Lk 5:4).

In addition, Pope John Paul II teaches that "[i]t is not enough to update pastoral techniques, organize and coordinate ecclesial resources, or delve more deeply into the biblical and theological foundations of faith. What is needed is the encouragement of a new 'ardor for holiness' . . . ." [1] As the book *In the Arms of Mary* testifies, it is our prayer life which renews and strengthens this desire in the midst of the many distractions and preoccupations of contemporary life. It is the development of our interior life which allows each one of us to focus our attention more clearly and decisively on God's universal call to holiness, to a sanctity which acts as the primary motivation and force behind the New Evangelization.

The graces God bestows upon us at our Baptism inspire us to grow constantly in faith, hope and love of both Christ and our neighbor. Yet, because of our weakness, we soon encounter struggles on our spiritual journey toward union with God. It is then that we must call upon God in humility with an ever deepening trust that the Lord calls us to Himself through our sanctification despite the fact that at times we may falter or we may become uncertain of His perfect will. Only when we respond to God's call to holiness by personal and intense prayer will our efforts to overcome "evil with good" bear fruit. As Jesus Himself reminds us: apart from Him we can do nothing.

I believe that *In the Arms of Mary* provides its reader with many profound and refreshing insights, based in Sacred Scripture, on how to deepen one's interior prayer life. It is a faithful companion piece to *The Gift of Faith*,[2] the widely acclaimed treatise on spirituality by Fr. Tadeusz Dajczer. Indeed, the author, Slawomir Biela, reminds us that our deepest longing for God's precious gifts of unconditional love and inner security cannot be fulfilled unless we continually renew our efforts to

---

[1] Pope John Paul II, Encyclical Letter: *Mission of the Redeemer (Redemptoris Missio)*, December 7, 1990, trans. "Vatican" (Boston, MA: Pauline Books and Media), 90.
[2] In Ireland known as *Inquiring Faith*.

discover the spiritual truth about ourselves through prayer. More importantly, God calls us to acknowledge who we really are – gradually to come to grips with various defense mechanisms and pretenses of our old self – without being afraid of His rejection or judgment, thus ripening within us the awareness that Divine Love, God's Merciful Love, overcomes everything.

In the face of the challenges to holiness which our age presents to individuals and to the Church at large, Biela follows the constant teaching of the Holy Father in emphasizing the important role of the Blessed Mother as the source of our hope. Through our imitation of Her humble, yet glorious example, we are given certain hope as we struggle to make progress on our path toward holiness. The author also reminds us in the examples of the Prodigal Son and the Canaanite woman that such a hope is found in humility and trust, where the acknowledgment of one's own smallness and powerlessness before God calls forth the outpouring of His redeeming mercy. In this sense, the thrust of the teaching of this book calls to mind that of Pope John Paul II *in Reconciliation and Penance*: ". . . we all do well to recall and emphasize the fact that contrition and conversion are even more a drawing near to the holiness of God, a rediscovery of one's true identity, which has been upset and disturbed by sin, a liberation in the very depth of self and thus regaining of lost joy, the joy of being saved, . . ."[3]

I am happy to be able to take this opportunity to support the apostolate of the Families of Nazareth Movement founded by Fr. Tadeusz Dajczer, the author of *The Gift of Faith*. This work,

---

[3] Pope John Paul II, Post-Synodal Apostolic Exhortation: *Reconciliation and Penance (Reconciliatio et Paenitentia)*, December 2, 1984, trans. "Vatican" (Boston, MA: Pauline Books and Media, 1984), 31-III.

which was translated into 46 languages, and the other books which focus on the same thrust of total self-abandonment in humility and trust to God and His mercy will continue to nourish the more than three hundred thousand members of the Families of Nazareth Movement across the world, and the many other souls seeking to be reassured of God's unconditional love and presence in their lives. I am pleased also to reaffirm my support to the vigorously expanding groups of this Movement here in the USA, where the number of the members has reached over three thousand and continues to increase rapidly throughout the country.

I am touched, in the work, by the author's openness and zeal in sharing with the reader his inner convictions and insights of God's amazing love and, in a special way, his reflection on the way in which the Blessed Mother lives so totally a life of trust. This small volume reveals Biela's fidelity to the motto "Totus Tuus Maria," even as we have seen it manifested so beautifully in the life of John Paul II. **In the Arms of Mary** is the fruit of the author's loving relationship with the Lord who gave us Mary, His Mother, to be our Mother. In Her loving arms and through Her humble example we, too, can become saints, who "virtually never grow old, . . ." and who "never become characters of the past, men and women of 'yesterday'. On the contrary: they are always men and women of 'the morrow', men of the evangelical future of man, and of the Church, witnesses 'of the future of the world'."[4]

† Theodore Cardinal McCarrick

---

[4] Pope John Paul II, Homily at Lisieux in front of the Basilica of St. Thérèse on June 2, 1980, "Fervent Communion with Christ's Sufferings," *L'Osservatore Romano,* In English (Vatican City), 23 June 1980, p.13.

Norberto Cardinal Rivera Carrera
Archbishop Primate of Mexico

A mong the roads that the Holy Spirit has provided for the renewal of the Church, one stands out: the insistent call for us to recognize the universal call to **holiness** for all the baptized. From Chapter V of the Dogmatic Constitution *Lumen Gentium* Vatican II,[1] to Chapter III of the Apostolic Letter *Novo Millennio Ineunte*[2] – not to mention other documents and voices of recent teaching – holiness is expressed (ever more as the days go by), as an urgent and pastoral priority; the foundation of all pastoral work. For this reason, it has been a constant preoccupation of the Holy Father to present new models of holiness to the contemporary world – drawn from the treasure of Holy Church – men and women who have opened themselves to the gift of

---

[1] Cf. Second Vatican Council, Dogmatic Constitution of the Church: *Lumen Gentium* (hereafter cited as *LG*), Solemnly Promulgated by His Holiness Pope Paul VI on November 21, 1964, trans. N.C.W.C. (Boston, MA: Pauline Books and Media, c.1998), V.
[2] Cf. Pope John Paul II, Apostolic Letter: *Novo Millennio Ineunte* (To the Bishops, Clergy, and Lay Faithful at the Close of the Great Jubilee of the Year 2000), January 6, 2001, trans. "Vatican" (Boston, MA: Pauline Books and Media, c.2001), III.

sanctity – men and women from every social condition, occupation and family situation, representatives from life's ordinary and extraordinary conditions, from different latitudes and cultures, those similar to us, like the people we live with in our daily life.

Holiness is not an extra, and even less, a resort for obtaining success in pastoral affairs. It is the same will of God, as Saint Paul reminds us: **"This is the will of God, your holiness..."** (1 Thess 4:3). This is the reason for our existence and the mission of the Church: full communion of men with God, our conformity with Christ, and through Him, to be introduced to the mystery of Trinitarian communion (see Jn 14-17).

Thanks to God, inadequate images and distorted stereotypes of holiness have begun to disintegrate, whereby sanctity was viewed as something for extraordinary men or women, "geniuses of holiness," and not the vocation of all the baptized who, having been incorporated into Christ, are called so that Christ's life may grow in them to the point of embracing them fully. Today holiness should be presented with adequate instruction since the roads to holiness are personal and therefore require an honest teaching of sanctity, capable of adapting itself to the pace of each person.[3]

We Mexicans have, in the events of Guadalupe, a magnificent example of an adapted and 'cultural' teaching. One of the first fruits of holiness stemming from the Marian pedagogy of Guadalupe can be seen in the Indian, Juan Diego, who has been offered today as a model of holiness – thanks to his canonization – to Mexicans and all men and women of the 21st century. Today we must place prominence in the events of

---

[3] Cf. *Novo Millennio Ineunte*, 31.

Guadalupe. That is to say, Mary's encounter with Juan Diego is an evangelizing and generating encounter of holiness, that is to say a privileged encounter with Christ.

Mary goes out to meet "Little Juan, little Juan Diego," as she called him from the very first apparition. This poor man, in the sense of the gospel, is someone open to God's love, which manifests itself to him in a special way through the love of Mary. She chooses him as her messenger or 'one who is sent', and as in every divine mission, the 'one who is sent' does not go alone, since the one who sent him goes with him. Holiness and mission are always personal, although they are founded on a universal vocation.

Juan Diego is for us an example of the way of faith and its trials. If being sent was already a trial of faith, the fatal illness of his uncle Juan Bernardino came as something "inopportune" at the critical moment of his mission: taking the solicited token to the Bishop. Nevertheless, confronted by his weakness, Mary does not abandon him. Finally it is she who goes forth to meet and comfort him, so that he abandons himself like a child in the arms of Mary.

Then, in spite of the weakness of his faith, and perhaps because of it, Mary reveals to him ever more fully, as his Mother, with such sweetness: "Am I not here, I who am your Mother? . . . Do you need anything else?" (NM 119). These words echo those which Our Savior addressed to Mary and John when they were at the foot of the cross "**...behold your son...Behold your mother**" (Jn 19:26-27). Juan Diego then, strengthened in his faith by Mary, entrusts himself to her, abandons himself to her, and goes off to fulfill her request. From that moment, Mary and little Juan Diego, just like Mary and John, begin a special communion of life together, on a special road to holiness. And just as St. John the

Apostle, in response to the testament of Christ **"...from that hour . . . took her into his home"** (Jn 19:27), Juan Diego also went to live with Mary. He not only went to live and serve in the hermitage that was built until the end of his life, but entered a special communion of life with Mary, which became his road to sanctification. He remained 'in the arms of Mary' in order to be guided to holiness.

Therefore, in good faith, I present and recommend this book *In the Arms of Mary*,[4] and although its theme is not about the events of Guadalupe, it is a timely aid to read and apply to our own lives that which is implicit in the encounter between the Mother of God and Juan Diego. In this way we can discover how Mary leads Juan Diego to a growth of faith and total abandonment to the love of The Blessed Mother, as if this were the pedagogy of Mary of Guadalupe on sanctification. It is necessary that we discover in the events of Guadalupe not only her choice of Juan Diego for a mission which was difficult for him, but also the preoccupation and action of Mary for the sanctity of the one who is sent.

In the Arms of Mary is a lucid, straightforward, and profound book. In it, the author examines step-by-step some elements of the road to holiness: prayer, its models, how to approach it through the ways of the Gospel. The road presented to us in this book nourishes us from the same source, delving in the same vein the Christocentric and Marian way which has nourished the spirituality and the Pontificate of John Paul II. Slawomir Biela, a Pole like the Pope, also portrays to us the

---

[4] Published in Great Britain and the United States as *Praying Self-Abandonment to Divine Love*, cf. Slawomir Biela, *Praying Self-Abandonment to Divine Love* (London: Science Press, 2002).

central landmarks of the life of her "who proceeds us on the pilgrimage of faith."[5] Mary is the indispensable aid and model on our journey through the darkness of faith until we come to live totally united with the will of the Father.

This book is in the same series as *Inquiring Faith*,[6] which is the spiritual bestseller of Father Tadeusz Dajczer, the founder of the Families of Nazareth (whose book has already been translated into 46 languages and among us issued in more than five editions). This Movement of Polish origin, which has spread throughout the world, has been a spiritual aid which feeds more than three hundred thousand people in the world and several tens of thousands in Mexico.

That our "Little Black Madonna of Tepeyac," who today elevates her little Juan Diego to the altars, may inspire those who imitate him, who without fear, and certain of being 'in the arms of Mary', may commit themselves to the work of New Evangelization with a new ardor of holiness.

† Norberto Cardinal Rivera Carrera

---

[5] LG 58.
[6] In the United States known as *The Gift of Faith*, cf. Father Tadeusz Dajczer, *The Gift of Faith*, 2d ed. (Ventura, CA: In the Arms of Mary Foundation, c.2001).

Ricard María Cardinal Carles Gordó
Archbishop of Barcelona

The reader has in his/her hands a deep book of spirituality. It is of the most genuine Christian spirituality because it reflects the works of the great doctors of the Church: St. Teresa of Avila, St. John of the Cross and St. Thérèse of Lisieux. Each of them is a master in the art of 'welling out of the well', an authentic Christian spirituality from the Gospel.

The author of this book on spirituality is a layperson. Slawomir Biela was born in Poland in 1956. He earned a doctorate degree in physics from the Warsaw University of Technology. It is surprising and full of hope that a scientist of our times such as he studied and in such a fruitful way, specialized in [the] theology of spiritual life at the Pontifical Faculty of Theology in the same city.

Since 1977, this author has collaborated with Professor Tadeusz Dajczer, the founder of the Families of Nazareth Movement, in the elaboration of the bases of the spirituality of this worldwide movement. The publications of the movement have been translated into many languages, including Catalan.

The book *In the Arms of Mary* [1] is the fruit of the author's fathoming the Christian mysteries. It shows the different stages of the interior life, and for this reason it becomes accessible for those who are at the beginning of the way as well as for those who have advanced deeper along the way of 'transforming union', as described by St. John of the Cross in his writings.

The book offers the same type of spirituality presented in the book written by Professor Tadeusz Dajczer, *Inquiring Faith*, [2] known all over the world and translated into over 40 languages. This work has been offered to the Catalan readers by the *Publicacions de l`Abadia de Montserrat*. I'm pleased to show my gratitude for offering to us also a Catalan version of this book on spirituality – a work written by a layperson.

Thanks to Baptism, Confirmation and their Christian vocation in the Church and in the world, lay people are also called to live deeply the ways of Christian spirituality and, in this sense, their testimony, their experience and – why not? – also their predicating can enrich and stimulate us, all of us, including those who have followed the way of the radical consecration to God in priestly ministry or in religious life.

Every one of us remembers the strong influence of the companionship and testimony of Jan Tyranowski in the life of the Holy Father John Paul II when he was young. Jan Tyranowski, a

---

[1] Published in Great Britain and in the United States as *Praying Self-abandonment to Divine Love*, cf. Slawomir Biela, *Praying Self-abandonment to Divine Love* (London: Science Press, 2002).
[2] In the United States known as *The Gift of Faith*, cf. Father Tadeusz Dajczer, *The Gift of Faith*, 2d ed. (Ventura, CA: In the Arms of Mary Foundation, c.2001).

layman, tailor by profession, was a mystic and he introduced him to the Carmelite spirituality, as well as to the young groups of the Living Rosary where his vocation as a priest was born. The remembrance of the 'mystic tailor' came to my mind during my reading the lessons of this 'mystic physicist'. May God wish to carry many along this path of deep spirituality, the only one that can give answers to spiritual hunger of many men and women of our times.

† Ricard María Cardinal Carles Gordó

Jaime Cardinal L. Sin
Archbishop of Manila

In the midst of confusion in today's world, we see souls desirous of serving God. So many people wondering what else they can do to offer themselves to God and to others. However, we also cannot deny that good will alone is not enough. We should desire not only to serve God, but to serve Him the way He wants to be served. For this to happen, one's main passion should be to constantly improve in interior life.

Why is prayer important? We can answer this question by analyzing the functions of prayer: Adoration, Contrition, Thanksgiving and Supplication. These we do when we pray. But what if we don't pray? Then it follows that we do not adore God, nor are we contrite for our sins, nor do we thank the Lord for His many blessings, nor do we ask Him for guidance and strength as we carry out our mission in life. In such a case, we are not at all doing God's work; rather, we are doing our work! Imagine, if we do not even ask God what His will is, how can we follow His will?

It is in this context that we can truly appreciate Slawomir Biela's book, *Praying Self-Abandonment to Divine Love.*[1] By abandoning ourselves to God's love through our prayer life, we can be assured not only of our desire to serve the Lord, but also of truly serving Him the way He wants to be served. Without prayer, we abandon ourselves to our likes and dislikes, to our opinions, to our whims. We become focused on our own capacities and intelligence, almost in the fashion of the New Agers who promote a "self-spirituality," instead of focusing on God's loving providence.

Let us turn to our Blessed Mother, as the author encourages us. Mary is our example of abandonment to God's will, as reflected in her life of holiness, faith, service, and humility. True devotion to our Beloved Mother cannot but surely lead us to her Son, Jesus Christ. Like her, may we always abandon ourselves in prayer, so that we may reflect God's love in our daily life.

† Jaime Cardinal L. Sin

---

[1] In the United States known as *In the Arms of Mary.*

Stephen Cardinal Kim Sou-hwan
Archbishop Emeritus of Seoul

In 1864, at the time of terrible persecutions in a village of Surich'igol near Kongu, Bishop Ferreol dedicated the young Korean Church to the Blessed Virgin Mary as the patroness. On the day of beatification of 103 Korean martyrs, John Paul II renewed this act in these meaningful words: *"I, John Paul II, once again entrust the people and the Church of this land into the loving care of Our Lady, the Mother of Jesus and of us all. Mother of all peoples and nations, you know all sufferings and hopes of every human person. As our mother you know the battle that goes on between light and darkness, good and evil, the battle that is fought in the world and in our hearts. Oh, Mother of Mercy, now I entrust to your loving heart all the people and the whole Church of this land."*

The papal act of entrustment brings back the first act of entrusting the humankind to Mary which was pronounced from the Cross by our Savior when he said: "Behold, your Mother!" Christ loved his merciful Mother with special love. John experienced, as we all do, a kind of perplexity and struggle within himself, a kind of battle fought between good and evil. He wanted to be faithful, however, he left his Master as others did. When he came back to the foot of the Cross, he was pardoned and given a gift. There was Mary, who entered his house, as well as his life, and thus his sonship was confirmed in a very special way. Her presence becomes an expression of the unfathomable mercy that God has for us "in whose souls the battle between good and evil continuously goes on."

The papal act of entrustment is still valid. It is both a gift and a calling to which we should respond. Our response can be given by means of our accepting Mary after the example of St. John. Life in communion with Mary leads to a profound life of faith, which reaches its fullness in our personal holiness. In this context, the book by Slawomir Biela titled *In the Arms of Mary* is of a great help to us. The author suggests a specific path to holiness that is possible for us to attain in our everyday life. He tells us that there are two abysses present in everybody's life. One of them is the abyss of our weakness, helplessness and sinfulness and the other one is the abyss of Divine Mercy. The former one, like a magnet, attracts the latter one, for this is the nature of God's fatherly love. We can accept God's love and His power only when we acknowledge our own weakness.

It is through prayer that we follow the path toward holiness, for it is through prayer that God leads us to discovering mysteries of the internal life. That is why this book by Slawomir Biela also teaches us how to pray. The prayer of the contrite taxpayer, the prayer of the trustful Canaanite woman and the prayer of the Good Thief show personal attitudes that, when adopted, open us up to God.

For many saints, their life in profound communion with Mary bore the fruit of being completely united with her Son. The one whose unique faith developed in everyday life becomes for us the Mother of our faith. After bringing Christ once into the world, she continues to give birth to Him in each one of us. A testimony given to such faith and communion with Mary could be seen in the martyrdom of thousands of our brothers. The Church in Korea that grew up on the soil sprinkled with their blood wants to follow the same calling to holiness to which they were faithful. I wholeheartedly recommend this book, hoping that for many of you it will be a precious help on your path to unity with God, no matter what stage of the spiritual journey you may be.

† Stephen Cardinal Kim Sou-hwan

THE NEW EVANGELIZATION

The Realization of the Universal Call to Sanctity

S t. Augustine states that on earth two great kingdoms exist, which will continue to exist to the end of time.[1] The boundary between them does not separate people or societies, as it runs through the center of every human soul. Two loves form these two kingdoms:

+ love of self to the point of contempt of God[2] and

+ love of God to the point of contempt of self.[3]

---

[1] St. Augustine *The City of God (De civitate Dei)* (trans. Rev. Marcus Dods, D.D. [New York, NY: Random House, Inc., 2000]) XIV, 28.
[2] *Amor sui usque ad contemptum Dei.* Ibid.
[3] *Amor Dei usque ad contemptum sui.* Ibid.

In the course of history, one gradually extends its border at the expense of the other. In the history of mankind, as in the life of each person, the objective is the building of God's Kingdom by bringing about the growth of Christ in each one of us. The acceptance or rejection of Christ defines the personal history of every human soul. John Paul II's call to the New Evangelization seems to take place in this context.

CHRIST GIVES US HIS MOTHER

Christ gives us His Mother as an example and special help in the building of His Kingdom and in continuing the work of evangelization of the world. Mary, who most perfectly bore witness by her life of faith, hope, and love, calls us to conversion and sanctification. No half-measures or compromises will transform the world, which in the process of secularization has strayed too far from the ideals of the Gospel. The work of the New Evangelization demands that we abandon ourselves totally to Christ following the example of Mary. The challenge of the present time and the current situation of the Church demand *radicalism of faith*.

The New Evangelization requires not only proclamation of the gospel, but first of all an authentic effort to pursue holiness by those proclaiming it. The Christian of the XXI century will be a mystic or will not be a Christian at all – as suggested by K. Rahner. John Paul II writes, "It is not enough to update pastoral techniques, organize and coordinate ecclesial resources, or delve more deeply into the biblical and theological foundations of faith.

What is needed is the encouragement of a new 'ardor for holiness' . . . ."[4]

The Second Vatican Council reminds us that radicalism of faith is impossible without radical conversion and fulfillment of the universal call to sanctity; otherwise, we will not become authentic witnesses of the Gospel. "Holiness, then must be called a fundamental presupposition and an irreplaceable condition for everyone in filling the mission of salvation within the Church."[5]

PRAYER IS A TESTIMONY OF CLOSE FRIENDSHIP WITH GOD

The Church always, but now particularly, needs saints – saints, who in the words of John Paul II, never grow old or become old-fashioned, forever remaining witnesses of the Church's youth.[6]

Our prayer, which should be our response to the universal call to sanctity, is fundamental for the New Evangelization. The efficacy of evangelization depends on prayer, in so far as prayer is an authentic expression of faith and love of God. "When prayer resulting from the stronger action of the love of God shows signs of a close friendship with God and reaches the point that it is a

[4] Pope John Paul II, Encyclical Letter: *Mission of the Redeemer* (*Redemptoris Missio*), December 7, 1990, trans. "Vatican" (Boston, MA: Pauline Books and Media), 90.
[5] Pope John Paul II, Post-Synodal Apostolic Exhortation: *The Lay Members of Christ's Faithful People* (*Christifideles Laici*), December 30, 1988, trans. "Vatican" (Boston, MA: Pauline Books and Media, 1988), 17.
[6] Cf. Pope John Paul II, Homily at Lisieux in front of the Basilica of St. Thérèse on June 2, 1980, "Fervent Communion with Christ's Sufferings," *L'Osservatore Romano*, In English (Vatican City), 23 June 1980, 13

relationship or union of love – the friendship then becomes an apostolic leaven . . . (cf. "The Way of Perfection" 32,12)."[7]

Stress on the value of prayer does not mean quietism. Love always demands a testimony of deeds. However, what is important is what lies at the heart of our actions. Trust in one's own strength prevents the realization of the universal call to sanctity. It is vital to search for God's will in a *spirit of evangelical humility*. Only the person who lives in a spirit of humility does not expect human recognition or visible results. He does not ask what stage he is at on his path to God. He accepts being left in darkness, unable to understand his experiences. Such a man is like a child, who in the darkness of the night holds on tightly to his father's hand. It is then that he begins to live in deep faith, dependent on his Heavenly Father for everything.

In order to keep a balance between these two poles – action and prayerful trust in God – which outline our path to God, it is necessary to undertake our actions as though everything depended on us, but at the same time, to trust as though everything depended on God. Nevertheless, in accordance with the divine economy, an economy of grace and mercy, our actions should flow above all from an interior disposition of the heart. Our commitment to the work of the New Evangelization should flow from this disposition. **Sanctity**, as St. Thérèse of the Child Jesus says, **is expressed most fully** not in actions or specific deeds, but in a **disposition of the heart**, which makes us **little and humble in the**

---

[7] "Saint Theresa of Jesus, a model and teacher of virtue [*Virtutus exemplum et magistra*] . . ." John Paul II, On the Occasion of the Teresian Year: "Pope's Letter to Superior General of Discalced Carmelites," *L'Osservatore Romano*, In English (Vatican City), 9 November 1981, 9.

arms of our Father, aware of our weakness and helplessness yet *trusting to the point of folly in His Fatherly love.*

The New Evangelization is being undertaken in extremely difficult circumstances, because it is directed toward a world penetrated by the breakdown of human and Christian values. The Church wants to remind contemporary man, who is incapable of renouncing himself and turning away from his egoism, about the *ideal of evangelical childlikeness.* The discovery that we lack the strength needed to live an ascetic life can lead us to an attitude of childlike humility and trust, which in turn attracts the power of God's Kingdom of grace. We need to be as small as a child in order to attract and be filled by the power of Divine Love, which is being bestowed upon the world. Evangelical childlikeness is expressed when we acknowledge the abyss of our littleness and helplessness. This attracts and summons the second abyss – the abyss of Mercy (*Abyssus abyssum invocat*).

In order for the New Evangelization to be an *ardent proclamation* of the Gospel to contemporary man, it has to be linked to the desire to live *The Beatitudes of Christ,* because they are the essence of the Gospel. This essence is most fully expressed by the beatitude: "Blessed are the poor in spirit..." (Mt 5:3). St. Augustine's contempt of self (*Contemptus sui*) is a form of *spiritual poverty,* which makes room for the Kingdom of love and grace – a place for the love of God. It is to the poor in spirit that the Kingdom of heaven was promised. Those poor in spirit are those who, not having anything, solely hunger for God.

The economy of grace, according to the teaching of the Council of Trent, is brought about through justice (*per justitiam*) and through mercy (*per misericordiam*). Our attitude toward God very often remains on the level of justice: I give to You, so that You give to me (*do ut des*). This comes from a conviction that man should earn God's love and that God gives us His gifts to the extent to which we offer ourselves, our work, and sufferings to Him. In the program of the New Evangelization, it is necessary, according to St. Faustina Kowalska's message, to pay particular attention to the *spirituality of mercy*.

A CHRISTIAN CAN ONLY RECEIVE SANCTITY FROM JESUS BY EARNESTLY ASPIRING TO IT

Contemporary man, while experiencing his helplessness, touched by suffering and perceiving how fruitless his efforts are, gradually comes to discover the existential truth: that he should abandon himself to the love of the Good Shepherd like the *helpless sheep*. A Christian should have a deep awareness that he cannot earn sanctity. He can only receive it as a gift from Jesus by earnestly aspiring to it. It is not we who give something to God, but God Who gives everything to us. Each of us will stand before God at the end of our lives with *empty hands*. Jesus Himself will come with His hands full to meet the man who has labored for God but remains before Him with empty hands.

God desires that we permit Him to manifest His love for us and, in response to His love, permit *Him to act in us*.

Our sinfulness does not stop God's action in us. By experiencing interior conflict as a result of sin, we can open up, like St. John the Apostle, who also experienced weakness and sin, to the words the Savior said to His beloved disciple and to all of us: "Behold, your mother" (Jn 19:27). John, entrusted then to the

Mother of God, "took her into his home." We, too, can discover in those words the call to self-entrustment to Mary as we invite her, who formed the earthly face of Christ, to form also this face in us. When we enter the communion of life with Mary, through self-entrustment to her, we also start on the path of fuller growth of unity with Jesus – on the path to holiness.

This book, *In the Arms of Mary*, ardently calls for a radical and total abandonment to Christ, because the world most of all needs saints to discover the Gospel again.

Rev. Tadeusz Dajczer

PART ONE

THE WAYS
THROUGH WHICH
GOD IS AWAITING US

When I was first given access to this formerly
inaccessible dwelling, where sovereign pontiffs
were said to live in frightening solitude, I was so
excited that I scarcely noticed, in the chapel with
the luminous crystal ceiling, a bronze Way of the
Cross on one wall and an icon of Our Lady of
Czestochowa on the altar. The Holy Father,
kneeling in prayer, looked huge. The cape on his
wide shoulders called to mind a snow-covered
landscape, and I wondered how it could have been
possible to get a mountain into such a small space.
(Since the attempted assassination of 13 May 1981
the snow will have melted to reveal the bare rock.)
I had before me a block of prayer. After Mass, said

1

quite meticulously and with the stately pace of an orbiting planet, twenty minutes was devoted to the thanksgiving, a practice almost obsolete elsewhere, during which John Paul II remained kneeling on his prie-dieu, the armrest of which is the size of a lectern. He prays, I am tempted to say as he breathes, and yet his prayer is action.[1]

Prayer is a search for God, but it is also a *revelation of God. . . . Through prayer God reveals Himself above all as Mercy* – that is, Love that goes out to those who are suffering, Love that sustains, uplifts, and invites us to trust. The victory of good in the world is united organically with this truth. A person who prays professes such a truth and in a certain sense makes God, who is *merciful Love*, present in the world.[2]

---

[1] André Frossard, *"Be Not Afraid!": Pope John Paul II Speaks Out on His Life, His Beliefs, and His Inspiring Vision for Humanity*, trans. J.R. Foster from French, N'ayez pas peur! (Garden City, New York: Image Books, 1985), 32.

[2] John Paul II, *Crossing the Threshold of Hope*, ed. Vittorio Messori, trans. Jenny McPhee and Martha McPhee (New York: Alfred A. Knopf, Inc., 1994), 25-26.

CHAPTER 1

TO PRAY WITH THE ATTITUDE OF THE TAX COLLECTOR

P rayer takes a very special importance among the different forms of man's meetings with God. It is in prayer, by raising up our thoughts to the Creator, that we are listening intently to His voice and searching for His will.

Don't we too seldom take advantage of this special way of being in such close contact with God? He desires that our whole life should become a constant prayer, lived in His presence and for Him.

Do you try every day to take time out from your daily chores to stand before God in the silence of your heart?

To enter into this silence and remain in it longer, try to clearly realize that:

> In this moment we are together – the 'I' and the 'Thou'.
> This is I, the sinner, before God who loves me.

'THE JUST' – BUT NOT JUSTIFIED

"He then addressed this parable to those who were convinced of their own righteousness and despised everyone else. 'Two people went up to the temple area to pray; one was a Pharisee and the other was a tax collector. The Pharisee took up his position and spoke this prayer to himself, "O God, I thank you that I am not like the rest of humanity – greedy, dishonest, adulterous – or even like this tax collector. I fast twice a week, and I pay tithes on my whole income." But the tax collector stood off at a distance and would not even raise his eyes to heaven but beat his breast and prayed, "O God, be merciful to me a sinner." I tell you, the latter went home justified, not the former; for everyone who exalts himself will be humbled, and the one who humbles himself will be exalted'" (Lk 18:9-14).

To whom is this parable directed? St. Luke says it clearly: "to those who were convinced of their own righteousness and despised everyone else."

> Jesus says to those self-righteous
> that, before God, they are in a situation
> much worse than the great sinners!
>> Before God, the recognition of the truth about ourselves
>>> is **that alone** which justifies us,
>>> and that means:

4

acceptance of our nothingness

always linked with trust in God's mercy.

Does this not surprise us? Why does God so easily justify the tax collector, a personification of sinfulness? Why does 'the just' Pharisee leave not only unjustified but with a promise of coming humiliations? Is it wrong if someone is not greedy, unjust, or adulterous, that he does not commit sins as grave as those of the tax collectors? Is it wrong of him to fast and pay tithes on everything he receives? Why then did the Pharisee go home unjustified?

What caused him to be so closed to the mercy of God?

In His parable about the Pharisee and the tax collector, Jesus explains this to us. Even the gravest sins do not close a man's heart to God as much as living a lie, that is:

failing to recognize one's nothingness,

glorifying oneself with the gifts God has given,

and considering oneself as superior to others on this account.

While the one who is justified is the person who confesses to God

his sins,

those committed in his thoughts, and in his words, in

what he has done, and in what he has failed to do[3]

and those sins from which God preserves him;

justified is he who makes an act of contrition

and, believing in God's mercy, prays:

"'Oh God, be merciful to me a sinner!'"

Frequently, people consider the Pharisee to be just, and the Pharisee considers himself as just. However, the advertence of Christ toward him is that he will be humiliated.

---

[3] Cf. Penitential Rite of the Roman Catholic Order of Mass.

If you begin to attribute to yourself the goodness which God bestows upon you, then you can be deprived of it.

THE THIEF OF GOD'S GLORY

The Pharisee was not a usurer, a cheat, an adulterer due in part to his cooperation with the grace of God. However, by taking credit for this for himself and lording it over everyone else, the Pharisee showed contempt for God.

This man robbed God of His glory, which belongs to Him alone, to build glory for himself. Therefore, he became conceited and that which was not his was the cause of his proud stance before God. What's more, because of God's graces, he was contemptuous of others. He did not stand before God in truth and did not admit his own nothingness. He failed to acknowledge the fact that he was capable of committing every kind of sin **if God did not preserve him** from doing so. The Pharisee did not admit to committing any sin. He failed to see his sins of omission and sins of squandering and misusing the graces of God. Thus he attributed everything good in his life to himself.

He was **unjust** toward God and toward those whom he held in contempt: those who were "greedy, dishonest, adulterous."

Did he, therefore, deserve to be justified in the eyes of Christ?
We, too, find ourselves in a similar situation –
when we come before God to confess a few 'little sins',
but we **omit with our silence** the vast abyss of our
      sinfulness:
      saying nothing about sins of omission,

about the sins of wasting graces,
about the sins which God continually
preserves us from committing.
God wants our justification,
but He will not call a person justified who does not want to recognize
his own nothingness
and who attributes God's gifts to himself.

YOU ARE ONLY A VESSEL

Putting yourself in God's presence, trust in His Mercy
and acknowledge the truth about yourself
as the tax collector did,
then God will look down on your wretchedness
and will have pity on you, His creature.
He will transform you,
will sanctify you,
and fill you with Himself.

If you want to imitate Mary's attitude and be like her, a vessel that God fills with Himself, then like her, you must be poor in spirit.

Even a vessel filled by God Himself can never forget that it is and will always remain a mere vessel. Here on earth the matter forming the vessel of our soul will always be as the tax collector described it: "'O God, be merciful to me a sinner.'"

We were sinners,
we are sinners,
and we will remain sinners to the end of our earthly lives.

7

"If we say, 'We are without sin,' we deceive ourselves, and the truth is not in us" (1 Jn 1:8). Even if we do not commit sins, while we are living our earthly life we continually have the capacity of sinning. Even if someone lives fully the teaching of Christ, he remains only a vessel – "that the surpassing power may be of God and not from us" (2 Cor 4:7).

TO PRAY LIKE THE TAX COLLECTOR

You should begin each day with the prayer of the tax collector. Every morning forget your feet and begin the day by kneeling before God for at least a few minutes – you cannot rush around the house first thing in the morning if you are on your knees. Your knees should remind you to pray and that you should do so with the attitude of the tax collector: "'O God, be merciful to me a sinner.'"

In the silence of your heart,
try to put yourself in the presence of God
with so much trust,
and recognize your sinfulness,
that which God permits you to perceive –
perhaps in relation to some sin
which is in your memory,
perhaps in the temptations that torment you.
Starting from this point,
try to elaborate on matters concerning your sinfulness...
As you become aware of some sin, confess it to God:
Lord, this is only one sin,
but I am capable of committing every conceivable kind of sin
if You do not preserve me from it.

Perhaps it might be easier for you to admit to your sinfulness,
when you recall the seven capital sins[4]
and the Ten Commandments of God.[5]

Praying in such a way with the prayer of the tax collector, you
will come to know what the vessel is really like – the vessel that
God made His temple.

The prayer of the tax collector will awaken **gratitude** in you
because He fills such a wretched vessel with Himself. You will
often repeat the words: *Lord, I do not understand Your love. I do not
understand that You want to remain in such a wretched vessel and to
come to such a great sinner – thank You for this.*

As often as you can, try to put yourself
before God's presence with the attitude of the tax collector.
Try above all during Holy Mass,
and when you receive Holy Communion.
But if you would participate in the Eucharist and receive the
Body of Christ with the hypocritical attitude of a Pharisee,
you would offend
God in a serious way.

---

[4] The seven capital sins are "pride, avarice, envy, wrath, lust, gluttony, and sloth or
acedia" as found in *The Catechism of the Catholic Church*, 1866 (1997).
[5] 1. I am the Lord your God: you shall not have strange Gods before me. 2. You shall
not take the name of the Lord your God in vain. 3. Remember to keep holy the Lord's
Day. 4. Honor your father and your mother. 5. You shall not kill. 6. You shall not
commit adultery. 7. You shall not steal. 8. You shall not bear false witness against your
neighbor. 9. You shall not covet your neighbor's wife. 10. You shall not covet your
neighbor's goods (see Deut 5:6-21).

Even the miraculous power of the Blessed Sacrament cannot transform a Pharisee because of his pride, unless he receives an efficacious grace.[6]

You must also pray the prayer of the tax collector in different moments of the day in ejaculatory form. Even for a moment, try to dwell on the thought:

> I have only my sins,
> but You love me Lord –
> thank You.

THE 'KISSES' OF SUFFERING

The ways in which God expresses His love for us
    can be totally incomprehensible for us.
Because, sometimes, He expresses his love
    with the 'kiss' of suffering,
showing us His particular trust,
and associating us in the mystery of His saving passion.
Painful humiliations can be expressions of His love;
loneliness,
accusations.
God's love for us can also be expressed

---

[6] The terms "efficacious grace" and "sufficient grace" are particularly related to the period of theological discussion about the efficacy of grace during the end of the 16th century. Without entering into this detailed theological discussion, it can be said that by sufficient grace (gratia sufficiens) we mean the "actual grace [temporary supernatural intervention by God to enlighten the mind or strengthen the will to perform supernatural actions that lead to heaven] considered apart from the supernatural effect for which it was bestowed. It may therefore mean the grace that does not meet with adequate co-operation on the part of the human recipient . . . ." "Efficacious grace (gratia efficax) on the other hand, is the actual grace to which free consent is given by the will so that the grace produces its divinely intended effect." Modern Catholic Dictionary (1999), s.v. "actual grace," "sufficient grace," and "efficacious grace."

by experiences **of darkness of faith,**
when suddenly you enter a state of dryness
and you are incapable of stirring a single positive feeling,
        even in prayer.
Then, in spite of your great efforts,
you are not capable of being good,
and you have the impression that,
instead of living the teachings of Christ more fully,
in reality you are no more than a caricature of a Christian.

Perhaps you may find this painful, but thanks to this, you discover with greater ease the truth about yourself. **You experience** that you are a sinner. This will form in you the attitude of the tax collector. These difficult experiences, which most of the time are beyond your understanding, can provoke your protest, perhaps even in rebellion. Do not be surprised that your ego will rebel because this is also part of the truth about you. Rather, you must be surprised when you do not rebel. Therefore, say: *God has given me the grace not to rebel.*

Indeed, this is a great and unmerited grace.

THE DISGUISED PHARISEE

It happens, however, that we are quick to attribute this grace to ourselves, and we begin to judge and lecture other 'rebels'. This is when the well-disguised Pharisee appears in us. Such a person deftly conceals his true face beneath a veil of false humility and diverse religious practices, which sometimes have been well practiced.

Perhaps someone may even praise you and may even take you as a model, but you remain being a Pharisee.

You will discover this only when you begin to pray the prayer of the tax collector. Do not be afraid to discover the abyss of your wretchedness; do not run away from what you see. This is the objective truth about yourself. If you wanted to live with the illusions, you would remain a Pharisee for the rest of your life on earth.

Not only should we begin each day with the prayer of the tax collector, but it should accompany us throughout the day. We soon forget this attitude of the tax collector, as we get caught up in the day's events. Our prideful self-assurance emerges in us once more. We still continue to put on new masks:

> one for the friends at work,
> one for the members of our family,
> and yet another for our confessor or spiritual director.

Sometimes we attempt to tear away one of these masks during confession and we only manage to remove part of it. And so our interior struggle continues. Even if our confessor tries to help us, he cannot do it for us. Since it is the penitent who has to confess and not the confessor, he has to respect our freedom. This interior struggle of pulling our masks off can be an extremely difficult trial. Some people fail many times. However, if they trustfully become open to God's mercy with no more human regard, they will someday discover the truth about themselves and will confess their sinfulness with complete sincerity.

They will then be truly touched by God

in the Sacrament of Reconciliation.
Do not be afraid of confession.
Remember that the best confession is when,
    with confidence, you reveal
        the abyss of your misery.[7]

Do not be afraid. The priest will not run away
        in horror at the sight of your sins,
and even if he did, God will not stop loving you.
You do not need to be afraid of God, because He already knows
        what is hidden within you.
Your only task is to be willing to be like the tax collector.
Trusting in God's mercy, you want to know
        what kind of vessel you are.

THE TWO ABYSSES

Do you want to know more deeply the extent of your own evil and at the same time the abyss of God's infinite love? Do you desire that your prayer may be converted more to that of the tax collector in the Gospel? If so, it is necessary that you put yourself more before the Cross.

    Looking at Christ nailed on the Cross,
    you will comprehend more easily
    how great an abyss[(7)] of evil your sins really are.
    Christ's suffering most fully reflects this abyss.

---

[7] The abyss is a symbol that represents an immeasurable reality, which does not have limits. For example, the abyss of sinfulness signifies the sinfulness of man whose profundity is realized through union with God. In this real situation it speaks about the abyss of spiritual misery, open to the redeeming love of Jesus, that is to say, the misery of man full of contrition before the Cross.

Standing at the foot of the Cross and adoring the One
    who took upon Himself all your sins,
you will come to know all the more fully these two abysses –
the abyss of your sin
and the abyss of God's love toward you.

The more frequently you put yourself in the presence of the
Cross, the more your attitude before God will resemble that of
the tax collector.

Because prayer at the foot of the Cross
deepens
the vision of one's sinfulness
as well as faith in the love of God.
Your evil was conquered and erased by virtue of the
    redemptive sacrifice of Christ.
Through the power of the One whose love for you has no limits,
    you were redeemed.
In adoring the Cross, you will realize this ever more fully.
    You can also pray in this way
        when you are before the Blessed Sacrament.
    In the Eucharist, in the Host that you adore,
    the glorified Christ is hidden.
    He was crucified, died, and is risen,
    in order to show you His love,
    a love that led Him to the Cross
    and led Him to become present in a small piece of bread.

THE WORLD PROCLAIMS THE TWO ABYSSES

It is insufficient that only during prayer we maintain the attitude
of a person who recognizes the abyss of his own sinfulness and, at

the same time, calls upon the abyss of God's Mercy. It is necessary to maintain this attitude throughout our daily life:

at work,

at home,

and, above all, in our contact with other people,

when we stand before our God

present in our neighbor.

Every person is a temple of God: "Do you not know that your body is a temple of the Holy Spirit within you, whom you have from God, and that you are not your own?" (1 Cor 6:19). When you are with someone, you can also adore Christ hidden within that person. The Holy Spirit and the crucified and risen Christ reside in every person. Once you remember this truth, you will start to perceive people in a different light.

The supreme and all-pervading love of Christ shown on the Cross can also be perceived in the whole of creation. It happened to St. Francis of Assisi who instantly tamed a wolf. This legendary story could be more than just a legend: St. Francis of Assisi obtained a miracle from the Creator by acknowledging the truth about himself and trusting in God's mercy. When the wolf unexpectedly extended its paw to St. Francis as a sign of friendship, the saint certainly did not attribute this to his good rapport with animals. Instead, he knew that that miracle was a fruit of God's omnipotence.

Always try to adore our Creator, present not only in another person but also in every creature, and thank Him for all of His deeds.

Everything that has been created reminds us of the Creator.
The whole universe speaks to us about God,
  who, in His Only Begotten Son,
    was crucified.

The trees, the flowers, the cornfields, the rocks, and everything surrounding you and serving you, proclaim God's great love for you. They resonate the love of Him, who continually bestows you with His gifts, despite your nothingness and your evil.

If you present yourself as frequently as you can before the Crucified Christ, you will be able to continually pray throughout the day the prayer of the tax collector. Thanks to this, the Cross will then become the center of your life – the Cross which encompasses the truth about God and about man. The Cross will draw you to live in the truth – and the truth will set you free (cf. Jn 8:32).

God, in seeing your humble attitude,
    can begin to work miracles in your life.
And He can even, perhaps, suspend the laws of nature!
If you become poor in spirit
and always remain in the truth before God,
believing in His omnipotence and love,
then everything in your life can change.
    You will begin to benefit from God's omnipotence.

THE PRAYER OF THE TAX COLLECTOR
– DIFFICULT AND DRY

The prayer of a person who is poor in spirit changes profoundly in accordance with the growth in interior life. Someone who experiences his first conversion will be able to pray the prayer of the tax collector without any great effort. God, then, touches such a person in a sensible way – such a person may even weep at the sight of his sins. This stage however, usually passes fairly quickly.[8]

Later on, your emotional contact with God will be interspersed with ever more frequent periods of dryness. At times you will have no problems with prayer, but at other times you will experience the inability to pray. Even if you want to pray like the tax collector, you will not feel like one. You will try to persuade yourself by force that you are a tax collector, but you will not be truly convinced that you are worse than anyone else, unworthy to "even raise his eyes to heaven" (Lk 18:13). The knowledge of the prayer of the poor in spirit will not be enough to change that which you feel.

This is normal.

Thanks to this, you will begin to perceive your insufficiencies
in the level of good will.

---

[8] "In Christian Life, four stages can be distinguished: that of the sinner, that of the converted Christian (beginner), that of the spiritual man (advanced), and that of the glorified or also transformed. It can be said that in the case of the first stage, the hardened sinner does not care about the commandments of God, neither about spiritual things. When some type of crisis comes about in his life, the first conversion is realized in him and he becomes a just man (man who lives correctly) or a Christian illumined by faith. St. John of the Cross does not treat (is not occupied by) the first conversion. He supposed that the reader already broke away from sin and from everything that would be an offense to God, and that it is less probable that he may return to these things." N. Cummins, *An Introduction to Saint John of the Cross*, (n.p., n.d.).

It is God who bestows the priceless grace of good will upon you. He wants you to accept this priceless grace, even though, in your freedom, it is possible to reject it. To be able to pray the prayer of the tax collector, you must admit that even your good will is not yours, but a gift received from the Lord.

Thanks to this dryness, your prayer will become more authentic. Then, by yourself, you will experience and understand that you have nothing:

You do not even know how to pray.

You are incapable of recognizing your sins.

You are incapable of standing in the truth.

And this is precisely the truth about yourself!

Once you discover this, it will certainly be difficult for you to persevere in prayer, recognizing that you are a sinner. You would prefer to finish praying as quickly as possible, justifying to yourself that to stay longer in prayer would be spiritual gluttony. Time for prayer therefore diminishes, and you try to convince yourself that you are merely not succumbing to spiritual gluttony. This is a typical rational mechanism of justification: trying to construct an additional theory that may justify your egoism.

ADMIT THAT YOU ARE INCAPABLE

When standing in the truth, you ought to admit that you reduce the time devoted to prayer because **you do not know how to pray, and furthermore, at times you do not even want to pray.** Usually, it is difficult for you to dedicate even a fragment of your time to God.

In spite of what you have discovered, try to talk
sincerely with Jesus:
Lord, You see that I do not know how to pray.
You know, Lord, that I do not have the attitude of the tax
collector —
contrite and trusting in Your Mercy.
I realize that every moment my thoughts are far from You.
Nevertheless, I believe that You will not reject me.
I believe that in Your presence
my seemingly useless efforts have value.

It is very important that you make the effort to continually
return to the attitude of the tax collector throughout the day and
when you are before Christ present in another person.

You will surely forget who you really are,
but you should not be angry with yourself for this.
You forget because you are a sinner.
Recognize that you are such,
and be grateful for God's
love with even greater fervor.
Thank Him for filling with His presence
such a wretched vessel.
Because in spite of your sinfulness, you are God's
temple —
in which He Himself wants to dwell.

To maintain the attitude of the tax collector is not easy. It
demands recognition of one's sinfulness in all situations of one's
daily life. To this end, a constant effort of the will is necessary. It
is most important to understand that you do not have to
emotionally feel that you are a tax collector.

Of what use is it that someone may be reduced to tears by having experienced emotionally one's sinfulness? In reality, one has only seen a small area of his sinfulness. Actually, emotion could have generated nothing more than a false belief that one prayed the prayer of the tax collector authentically, and can intensify such illusion that one has known fully the truth about oneself.

It is better then to recognize in the presence of God
that you are incapable
of becoming like the tax collector.
What is most important is not to be afraid to stand in the truth.
Do not be afraid to speak with God
with full sincerity about your wretchedness.
With this, you express your trust toward Him.
You will also know what it is to experience peace and interior joy,
you will experience the freedom of the heart
and you will begin to be happy –
because life lived in the truth leads to this.
The tax collector does not know if he was justified and accepts it.
The Pharisee, however, was convinced that he was 'just'
during, as well as after, prayer.

If, after praying, we think that we have an authentic prayer of the tax collector and that we already know the truth about ourselves, we would be demonstrating the attitude of the Pharisee who is satisfied with himself.

Let us not deceive ourselves. We will always have the attitude of the Pharisee to a certain degree. Our knowledge of the confession of our sinfulness will always show a small fragment of the objective truth. It is not likely, here on earth, that we are capable of standing fully in the truth before God. Only in heaven will we stand fully in the truth before Him – face to face. "At present I know partially; then I shall know fully, as I am fully known"(1 Cor 13:12).

The saints, too, learned the truth about themselves gradually. We do not know if, while on earth, they knew the truth in its totality.

We do not have to deceive ourselves in thinking that someday here on earth we will know the whole truth.
Nevertheless, such truth must be wanted and begged for ardently by us. It will not be an error if we are always convinced that we only see a small part of the truth about ourselves.
A constant dissatisfaction of standing
in the truth before God
should always accompany your prayer.
This should be accompanied with the conviction that:
I am like a pharisee,
even if I already know my nothingness and sinfulness,
it is only to a minimal degree.
We should question ourselves before Him
with admiration:
Lord, how can You love someone who is a hypocrite
and liar
through and through;
to love someone like me is a folly!
Here on earth, we will never comprehend the paradox that such an abyss of misery and sinfulness can be filled with the abyss of God's love.
The discovery of this truth should always be accompanied
by admiration –

21

the awe and wonderment at the folly of God's love for us,
that we are an abyss of nothingness and of sinfulness.

WHEN NO PROGRESS IS VISIBLE

The struggle of dying to oneself and against one's weakness can be compared to one's effort of scooping up water with a bottomless glass: the constant repeated efforts do not produce any result. Similarly, you too will see no progress at the beginning. You may become angry with yourself. Perhaps in the state of discouragement, you may say: It is not possible that I can be faithful to God.

It is true, because it is not possible for you to be faithful to Him by your own forces.

Nevertheless, you must struggle
until the moment when, with awesome wonder,
you will notice
that the water does not spill from the bottomless glass!
This will be the moment when God begins
to work miracles in your life.

However, before this happens, it must be clear to you that you are incapable of bringing about any supernatural good on your own. Such clarity is not just affirmed in theory. You must really **experience and recognize** this truth after countless and repeated attempts of scooping up water with the bottomless glass.

God will then have compassion on you.

However, it would be fatal, if after such a special intervention of God in your interior life, you would say:

At last, I am good.

It took a long time, but at last, I am a good father,

a good mother,

a good worker,

and my confessions are better and better.

If this were to happen, you would have to begin all over again, until you experience once more that:

by yourself, you are incapable of doing any supernatural good.

Because you are not capable,

you simply have to make every effort to live according

to the Gospel. You should do everything that you can

until the moment comes when God performs the miracle.

It happened, too, with St. Thérèse of the Child Jesus. She also struggled against her weakness for many years. And finally, God worked a miracle: she began to live fully the teachings of Christ. She was really convinced, however, that it was due to God and His mercy.

You will also have to struggle against yourself for many years, until finally, **God** will make it happen, and you will begin living like the tax collector.

And then you will really become a good father,

a good mother,

a good Christian –

through God's Mercy.

It will be necessary for you to believe

that one day God will perform the miracle –

He Himself will do in you everything

that you cannot do.

CHAPTER 2

THE MEETINGS WITH GOD

In practical daily life, prayer is generally connected to many difficulties.

It demands not only the involvement of our will and reason but also demands our total surrender to God.

Perhaps you dedicate very little time to God, using every obstacle for your justification. Perhaps you believe that you cannot concentrate on God whenever more distractions appear, and your prayer is not as emotionally charged as it used to be. Perhaps, by deceiving yourself, you give up too easily any effort to enter inner recollective silence.

By giving up any effort to remain in a more profound prayer of recollection, you are at the same time renouncing a very important form of your encounter with God –

a form which is one of the most important ways to meet God.

To avoid this, try to utilize in your prayer certain symbols and images pertaining to God.

FINDING ONESELF IN THE HEART OF CHRIST

To find oneself in the heart of another is similar to that of a mother who accompanies her child with her thoughts and lives the life of her child. So God, too, but in an incomparably greater degree, carries the whole world in His heart. He takes care of everything that we need, most especially everything we need for salvation. The Creator of the world loves the work of His creation. God looks at each one of His children with infinite love and care. He bears the whole of humanity in His heart, keeping every single one of us in His thoughts, and immerses us in the fire of His love.

Finding oneself in the heart of Christ can be a form of meeting with God and of deepening the mystery of His love for you.

During His suffering on the Cross, Christ gathers all people in His heart:

> sinners and saints,
> good and evil,
> believers and unbelievers.
> Jesus Christ desires to immerse and purify everybody
> in the love of His Most Sacred Heart.

The burning fire of love in the heart of Jesus can purify the entire human race; it was by this love that all of us were redeemed. But not everybody wants to receive this love.

You too have a special place in the heart of Jesus – with all your sins and unfaithfulness. It is the heart of Jesus, pierced with the lance and surrounded by thorns, that embraces you in an unfathomable love. But you, like that thorn and lance, numerously pierce through His heart. Christ, nonetheless, still keeps you in His heart. If He would remove you from it – you would die. Jesus also immerses in His love all those who do not believe in Him and those who hate Him, for otherwise they would cease to exist. All of us remain in His heart because we are all children of God.

By meditating on this mystery, you will find your place in the Church – the People of God, redeemed and immersed in the heart of Jesus.

> The heart of God burning with love is a place of our refuge,
> it is the place where we are free and safe.
> It is like a fortress,
> where God protects each one of us.

You are the one who is capable of not wanting to remain in this heart. You have been gifted with free will. By rejecting the teaching of Christ, you are not wanting to recognize God the Father. In spite of this, God never rejects you.

God is **defenseless** in His love for you. That is why, because of this, you can wound Him very deeply. You are His child, and you have a right to be in the Divine heart, but also by being His child, you can wound Him most painfully.

> The greater the awareness and willfulness of your
> unfaithfulness to God's will,

the more consciously and willfully you wound Him.
By meditating on the truth of your presence in the
heart of God,
you can come to know more fully the truth about His love
and the truth about your sin.

You cannot fully be a disciple of Christ if you do not believe that, because of your sinfulness, you are immersed in the love of His heart. If you do not have faith in His love, you will have insufficient motivation to live out the Gospel. Only when you believe that you are loved will you adapt, in the face of overwhelming difficulties, the attitude of a child, who with trust, presents oneself before its Father. You will then find the courage to learn in a deeper way about the abyss of your own wretchedness.

At the root of all evil is your ability to say NO to God.
Being free, you can reject His love.
It is possible for you not to believe that you have been called
to a life in God,
and that through Him, you have been called to that eternal love
in the life to come.

If your faith becomes weaker, try to find yourself as frequently as possible in the heart of God:

during moments of prayer,
in every moment of your daily life, and
above all, when you feel crushed
by the weight of your worries,
and the burden of carrying them seems pointless and
hopeless.

Nothing is hopeless
for the one who believes that he is in the heart of God.

Faith in God's love will permit you to understand that everything that happens to you is grace.[9]

As long as you live, God continually bestows you with countless graces. Nevertheless, you will be obliged at the moment of your death to make a definitive decision – either you believe in God's love and accept it or reject it for all eternity.

The thought of death should not frighten you too much. For it will only be a bodily death that has to happen. You will rise again.

At the moment of death, when you present yourself before God
with empty hands, you can resort to God's love with childlike trust.
Thanks to this trust – which will be formed in you throughout
your entire earthly life –
you will become open to the grace of salvation.

IN HIS WOUNDED ARMS

Another way you can encounter God, which can help you to be immersed more deeply in the awareness of the mysteries of His love and your sinfulness, is for you to discover the truth that you are held in the arms of Christ.

Jesus holds you in His arms,
similar to a father and a mother who embrace their beloved child.

---

[9] St. Thérèse of Lisieux, *Her Last Conversations*, Jun. 5, no. 4, trans. John Clarke, O.C.D. (Washington, DC: ICS Publications, 1977), 57.

He embraces you with His hands, which were nailed to the Cross for the sake of your salvation. With His arms outstretched on the Cross, He says to you: I love you, I offer my life for you, so that you can be saved.

> Nevertheless, you are free –
> you can freely remain in the arms of Christ,
> but you can also escape from them.
> With His gesture of open arms for you, Jesus does not enslave you, He simply **expresses His love for you.**

Is it not the case that you despise this gesture of love in the name of independence so fomented by your egoism?

> By escaping from the arms of Christ, you inflict new pain on Him. When you try to escape by deciding your own destiny by yourself, you are making a decision
> of living life as if God does not exist.
> The Creator, who with great love, holds
> in His hands the entire universe,
> and sustaining thus its existence,
> also holds you, who are mere dust, with the same kind of love.
> As a creature, you are undoubtedly dust,
> but it was God who created you
> and for Him you are someone exceptionally loved –
> someone unique.

In moments of most difficult trials and darkness of faith, do not forget that you are held in the arms of God Himself.

The hands of Christ are the hands of a paternal and maternal love, for God's love combines together fatherly and motherly love.

Christ holds you in His arms because you are His beloved child, but remember that He is experiencing extreme pain. It was for the sake of your salvation that He was scourged, crowned with thorns, nailed to the Cross, and His heart was pierced by a lance.

When you try to break away from His arms,
Jesus retains you
at the cost of His wounds being reopened.
When you struggle with the attitude of escaping from Him,
because you refuse to believe in His love,
once again blood flows from His wounds.
With this blood, you will be cleansed from your sins —
if you return.
Do not escape.
Believe that your salvation is in Christ alone.

You can reflect on the truth about the unfathomable love of God not only during times set aside for prayer but also when you find yourself in the company of another person. It is impossible to know the full depth of the mystery of God's love for us here on earth, but certain images can help us become closer to such truth.

In the later stages of interior life, God may give you the ability to come to know His love in a different form and in a more fruitful way. However, before such a different experience of His love is bestowed on you in such stages, God expects that **you persevere in prayer**. Thanks to persevering in prayer, you will already know, to some degree, your wretchedness and the greatness of God's love.

BEFORE THE CRUCIFIED CHRIST

The Christ who is present before you during prayer is the Christ of Mount Tabor, full of majesty and power; but He is also the Crucified Christ.

If you pray before Him who was crucified for and because of you, He Himself will teach you the fundamental truths of Christianity. You will then understand that Divine justice is different from human justice.

Jesus, before "his hour" (Jn 13:1) came, had already foreseen the immense suffering He would have to undergo by which He would be crushed for the sins of the world, despite being innocent. He saw our sins and faults which, through the will of the Father, He would have to take on Himself. He knew perfectly well that He was going to be rejected by men,

He would be mocked and spat upon,
scourged and crowned with thorns
and, with immense cruelty,
He would be tortured to death on the Cross
like the worst criminal –
and Jesus accepted everything.

In the garden of Gethsemane, He fell on His face and was humbly praying: "'My Father, if it is possible, let this cup pass from me; yet, not as I will, but as you will'" (Mt 26:39).

By praying before the Crucified Christ, you will receive the answer to the question: Why do I suffer injustices in my life? You will understand that God can permit something unjust, from a human point of view, to happen to you – because God sees things differently than men. The human injustice that you confront may be something just in God's eyes. As a sinner, all you deserve is rejection and punishment.

When you do not experience any injustice, you cannot understand with depth what Christ went through, whose death also had something to do with the injustice He experienced.

Someone who is condemned justly - like the good thief - can find a rational motive to accept suffering. However, someone who is unjustly accused and suffers despite his innocence, can only turn to the Cross of Christ for his motivation. Only when you resort to the Cross of Christ can you be grateful for the injustice that you suffer:

I give thanks to You, my God, for sharing with me
Your most precious treasure.
Thank You for permitting me to understand better the mystery of
Your Cross.

On your way to sanctity, you may not expect that God will preserve you from injustice, and that nothing will happen to you, from a human point of view, that you do not deserve.

St. John the Baptist, who proclaimed the truth and called the people to conversion to prepare for the coming of the Messiah, did not deserve death in the light of the law. It was the whim of Herodias which caused him to be killed. From the human point of view, John the Baptist suffered a great injustice. Yet God, in the inscrutable designs of His Providence, permitted it.

A HIDDEN GIFT IN EVERY EXPERIENCE

In all your experiences, even those which you do not understand, God conceals some special gift for you. You will understand this as you pray before the Cross and immerse yourself deeply in the mystery of the actions of God.

> When you are crushed by suffering
> and suffer some injury,
> you become closer to the Crucified Christ.

Your cross enables you to be more united with the Crucified Christ, and it helps you understand in a deeper way the mystery of Christ's passion, death, and resurrection. Therefore, do not be surprised to encounter one suffering after another or to be rejected more often by people.

> The thought of suffering is horrifying,
> but, in fact, this was the way of Christ.

In the light of faith, you will understand that the greatest distinction that you can receive from Him, is when Christ shares His suffering with you –

> that it is the suffering of someone
> condemned unjustly,
> ridiculed,
> and tortured to death on the Cross.

Jesus accepted this suffering as a sacrifice for your sins. If you want to be more like Him, it is necessary that you take advantage of this sacrifice in the fullest possible way. By praying before the

Cross, you will begin to discover the true **immensity** of the love of someone who accepted a disgraceful death on the Cross in order to save **you**.

The Crucified Christ calls you to imitate Him,
that in His attitude of total obedience to the Father,
you may find a model of life and example
to base your life upon.

Difficult experiences, trials of faith, or the problems of daily life will always be hard to bear. It is possible that your cross may have new situations that can afflict you,

lack of strength, lack of rest,
a pile-up of new obligations,
a responsibility that crushes you.

All of these can become very difficult experiences, but in the light of faith, Christ's yoke is easy and His burden light. Your cross permits you to unite yourself with the Crucified Christ. Therefore, try to look at all your difficulties and experiences with peace and trust.

You are not alone on the way of the Cross.
Mary also went along the same way.
She partook, in a spiritual form, that which Jesus experienced –
from the garden of Gethsemane up to the Cross.
She, who most faithfully followed Her Son
through the way of the Cross,
is now with you.

Without doubt she would like to say to you: Courage! Do not be afraid. The way through which you tread leads you to salvation and sanctity.

BEFORE CHRIST WHO IS FULL OF POWER

In your prayer, you are usually before the Christ of Mount Tabor, before the One who has the power to perform miracles and overcome all evil.

Perhaps, at these times, you behave as did St. Peter. Perhaps, like him, you are astonished when you witness that Jesus transforms someone's heart or cures someone. These signs are for you a testimony that Christ is with you.

May they remind you of His omnipotence,
that on your way to union with the Crucified Christ
they may fill your heart with peace.

CHAPTER 3

DESCENDING IN THE SILENCE OF MEDITATION

M editation is the process by which we actively try to fathom certain truths and divine mysteries through our reason, imagination, and affections.

Different methods of meditation have been devised within the Church, many of which have been accepted and approved. It is therefore proper, and often recommended by the Church, to use these classical methods. However, the search for different forms of prayer should not be forgotten. Just as prayer is a continual process, so a search for one's own path leading to God is a process.

While searching for the path on which God waits for us, we can try to supplement classical methods with practices to which our heart is inclined.

When the Lord permits us to pass from one stage of interior life to another on the way to sanctity, it is essential to put aside certain common methods of meditation. To remain bound to one method could disturb the free actions of the Holy Spirit.

CHRIST BEFORE YOUR EYES

When you are preparing for meditation,
try to quiet yourself down in a profound manner
so that you can put yourself in God's presence,
– the Father who is all-embracing Love –
in the silence of your heart.
Read the text from the Sacred Scripture or from some
appropriate text,
and begin your meditation.
Now it is important to make yourself aware
that it is Christ
– before whom you are present –
who is addressing you,
that it is He who pronounces the words,
        which will be the content of your meditation.
The selected text is the living word of God addressed to you,
despite the fact that of yourself you are dust and ashes before Him.

When Abraham intercedes before God for Sodom and Gomorrah, he says: "'See how I am presuming to speak to my Lord, though I am but dust and ashes!'" (Gen 18:27).

Abraham believes in God, who embraces him with His love, because he daringly asks God to change His plans. At the same time, however, he is aware of the great difference that distinguishes him from God, and therefore stresses "'I am but . . . ashes!'"

The words: "'Since I have thus dared to speak to my Lord'" (Gen 18:31) give witness to his attitude of profound respect toward God.

God demands the same attitude from Moses when He reveals Himself in the flames of the burning bush: "So Moses decided, 'I must go over to look at this remarkable sight, and see why the bush is not burned.' When the Lord saw him coming over to look at it more closely, God called out to him from the bush, 'Moses! Moses!' He answered, 'Here I am.' God said, 'Come no nearer! Remove the sandals from your feet, for the place where you stand is holy ground . . .' Moses hid his face, for he was afraid to look at God" (Ex 3:3-6). What does the order to take off the sandals mean? God tells Moses that he must adopt an attitude full of respect before the Creator and also in the place where God reveals Himself to him. Upon becoming aware that he is in the presence of God, Moses covers his face; in this awesome moment, he experiences his own nothingness. At the same time, however, he experiences God's love, because in spite of his fear, he does not run away.

If, when in prayer, you do not experience this extraordinary nearness of God, as happened in the case of Abraham or of Moses, it means that God waits for you to have faith. Christ wants you to believe that, although you cannot feel Him, He is with you. He wants you to believe that He is before your eyes even if you may not see Him.

The first stage of meditation consists
of putting oneself before Jesus,
and listening attentively to the words
that He tells you.

While persevering in the presence of Jesus, try meditating on His words, penetrating their depth and meaning.

These are the words of someone who died for you on the Cross. Thus, you can imagine that Christ addresses them to you from the Cross – He utters them looking at you with love, despite your sins which nailed Him to the Cross.

So that it may be easier for you to remain in the presence of the Crucified Lord during your meditation, you may have a Cross in front of you. For some, the Cross alone will already be a meaningful sign, whereas for others, it will be conducive to prayer, a clear image of Christ crowned with thorns, with all the wounds and His pierced side.

Stand in the truth before Christ.
Believe that He directs His words to you,
in spite of your continuous inattentiveness to them,
just like the evangelical "swine,"[10]
            you are ready to trample on them.
Try, then, to confess to Christ that which
you become aware of:
> **Lord, I don't understand why,**
> **in spite of me being so closed,**
> **You want to speak to me.**

---

[10] "Do not . . . throw your pearls before swine . . ." (Mt 7:6).

In fact, You know before whom You cast the pearls
of Your words.
Thank You for still wanting to talk to me in spite of this.

CHRIST IN YOUR HEART

Christ in your heart is telling you
His words from the text, which is the content
of your meditation.
He not only speaks them **to you**
but He also speaks them **in you** –
because He lives in you.
These words ought to become part of your 'self'.
They should penetrate the deepest layers of your personality.
They are living words and are full of priceless gifts for you,
because through them special graces are connected.
    The meditation will help you to delve deeper into the truth
    that you are never left alone –
    because in the "earthen vessel" (cf. 2 Cor 4:7) that you are,
    Christ dwells.
    He chose this 'vessel' in order that it would be His temple.

In fact, you are a child of God; further, you became His child by the grace of Baptism and also by the graces of the other sacraments. Therefore, through them, you know that God dwells in you – you are His temple. By receiving the body of Christ, you become a living liturgical custodian and you yourself become like a living tabernacle. Not only do you become His temple during those particular times; rather, you are always His temple.

Do you show due respect to God who chose you as His home?

When do you have, to at least some degree, the posture of the lifeless temple walls, which with majestic dignity protect Christ, hidden in the Blessed Sacrament?

Do you adore God who is within you?

Do you try to remind yourself of His presence, not only when you pray but also in the ordinary moments of your life? The greater the intensity you live with this awareness, the more fervently you will try to make room for Him in your heart.

> As fruit of this reflection,
> an awareness will come about
> that by your sins and infidelities,
> almost every instant,
> you offend Him.

You will begin to notice that in actual fact, you, who are the living temple of God, are more occupied by your idols and by your daily preoccupations than by God.

> Your distractions during prayer are proofs that this is true.
> They show you that your daily concerns
>   fill your heart more than God does.
> They prove that there is no faith in you,
>   such truth would allow you to be detached from them.
> In this manner, the freedom of heart may grow in you,
>   in order that it may be truly filled by God alone.

The temple of God is a holy place, and you make of it such a 'marketplace' of your own lust and of your daily preoccupations, that you do not want to trust God. By your sins and continuous infidelities, it is a miserable place and perhaps even filthy. Nonetheless, you continue to be the temple of God and you will remain so until the end of your life.

> Against all logic,
> Christ deposits
> the treasure of His word
> precisely in this filthy vessel,
> even though He knows that you can reject it.
> Therefore, remaining in the presence of Jesus
> who made of your heart a temple of God,
> be joyful for the unfathomable love He shows you.
> When you come to acknowledge the truth before Him,
> you can say to Him:
>> Lord, You know that this vessel is incapable
>> of using the treasure You put in it.
>> In this moment, I want to live according to the words
>>> that You address to me,
>> but only because I abound in feelings and emotions.
>> Nevertheless, You, more than anybody else, know very well
>> that when this passes,
>> I won't be able to live according to Your word,
>> because it is beyond my capabilities.
> And in this way, you can meditate for some time:
>> on one side,
>> on the great love God has for you,
>> and on the other,
>> on your wretchedness.

You can have the interior experience of this admirable presence of God with strong emotion. However, it may also be that you meditate on His presence in the state of great dryness. Then, the only expression that you are aware of being a 'temple of God' may be, for example, the repetition of the prayer of thanksgiving:

Thank you, my God, for Your presence in my heart.

It is not necessary that this expression of gratitude be accompanied by an emotional experience, and at times it may seem to you as a 'mechanical prayer'. Nevertheless, the expressed prayer of gratitude in the midst of dryness can express the required disposition of your **intellect** and your **will**.

God focuses on the disposition of intellect and will.

Even if you are completely empty and incapable of feeling anything, you can say to God:

Thank You for being in my heart,
in spite of my emptiness
and incapacity of anything.

Through His Redemptive Sacrifice on the Cross, Christ obtained for you this inconceivable grace whereby God makes you His temple.

Thus, you can say
that the **Crucified Christ** resides in your heart
crucified by your sins.
It is necessary that Christ's Cross be deeply carved in your heart.
While adoring the Crucified Christ
ask pardon from Him, because with your sins and infidelities
you continuously crucify Him –
while at the same time, thank Him for having obtained for you
the grace of salvation.

CHRIST IN YOUR HANDS

At a further stage of meditation,
you can assume
that the words you read were placed in your hands
like a Host,
in the similar way that the priest places the Host there.
They are **filled with God's presence.**

God entrusts Himself into the dirty hands of a sinner by placing these words in your hands – the infinite love that He has for you touches the abyss of your nothingness.

Christ wants to entrust into your hands the precious pearls of His word, even though you immediately forget the content of your meditation, and like the evangelical "swine,"[10] you can cast this treasure under your feet and trample on it.

Once you realize how deeply you wound God with such an attitude,

put yourself before Him – contrite and repentant
and at the same time, thank Him
for His infinite mercy.

For in His mercy He forgives you of every evil for which you are contrite and repentant. He also forgives you for continually disregarding and wasting the gift of His word.

By acknowledging the truth before God, you can ask Him:
My God, grant that I may not scorn Your gift.
I beg You for the miracle
of my being open to Your word,

for the grace of accepting Your gift
and for the grace of living according to Your word.
The chosen text is a call
to attentive and profound reflection about yourself,
to penetrate all layers of your misery,
in order to present it to God with a contrite heart.
Recognize your sins and infidelities,
then trust in the Divine Mercy
and give thanks to God for His inconceivable love
toward you.

He gives you the right to Redemption through His death on the Cross. Christ puts in your hands the right that He obtained for you in order that you yourself may be disposed to it. You can take advantage of it, but you are not obligated to it, in the same manner that you may or may not resort to Divine Mercy.

When He places in your hands the gift of redemption,
He puts Himself in your hands.
He is made defenseless in your hands like a Host.

It is as if He would say to you: I am in your hands, you can do with Me whatever you would like.

This is the unfathomable mystery of the love of God –
who did not only die for you but also is offered at
your disposition.
He loves you,
but respects very much your freedom,
which permits that you can waste it.
He pours over your hands torrents of graces,
but He permits you to make of them that which you want.

Generally, these graces are wasted as they escape through your fingers, and you take advantage only of a few drops of graces that remain in your hands. Those graces which were not accepted are **sins of omission**. Only Christ knows how many sins of omission there are in your life. He knows it, and, in spite of this, He continuously pours into your hands the richness of His graces! When you begin to take notice of the quantity of your wasted graces, it may frighten you, but then you will understand better that you can be saved thanks to the Redeeming Sacrifice of Christ.

> By meditating on the presence of Christ in your hands,
> you will understand someday
> that you have in them the Crucified One,
> whom you yourself crucify
> when you waste the graces that He offers you
> and you do not receive them.

Therefore, you will comprehend that it is **His blood which escapes through your fingers**, because by not receiving His graces you reject His gift of salvation.

Christ expects that someday you may understand all of this, and that you may be converted; that someday you will want to benefit from His Redemption. If you frequently become aware of how you treat God, who is offered in your hands, then, certainly, repentance for your sins including those of omission, will be born in you. At the same time, gratitude for Redemption will be born in you. This will be a motivation for a fuller response to the graces placed in your hands; graces with which you should cooperate.

Do not be discouraged by the sight of the vast number of graces that you waste. Believe that Christ also redeemed the sins of omission. When the Apostles asked: "'Then who can be saved?' Jesus looked at them and said, 'For human beings it is impossible, but not for God. All things are possible for God'" (Mk 10:26-27).

Looking at your spiritual situation only from a human point of view can lead you to despair or to total indifference. So it is necessary that you also see your innumerable sins of omission in the light of faith. **The most important thing is to believe in the love of God.** He loves you in spite of all your misery.

Christ will begin to transform you only if you have a faith and trust beyond the cost of everything. Therefore, trust that "God is love" (1 Jn 4:8).

Only a heart that loves can notice that it is gifted.

A bride, when she is in love, perceives even the smallest expressions of love from her bridegroom, even if they are only expressed through the most common and ordinary gestures.

So it should be between yourself and God. However, it is arrived at only through trustful and persevering prayer.

ENDING YOUR MEDITATION

In the final part of meditation
you can make a concrete resolution,
expressing it in the form of prayer:
Lord, thank You for permitting me to understand more fully

the mystery of Your love.
You never stop loving me.
I believe that, when with a contrite heart I confess
my sins,
You forgive me for everything
and like the lost sheep You take me and You carry me on
Your shoulders.

In ending your meditation
return once more to the great mystery that:
you are in Jesus' heart,
and you are in Jesus' arms.

You must desire to live with the awareness of God's unfathomable love for everyone, including those who reject Him. Through faith in this unfathomable love, you will be uniting yourself to Jesus in your daily life, and you will respond to the greatest desire of His heart: that everybody may believe that "God is love" (1 Jn 4:8).

Go out and meet the desire of the heart of Jesus.
Do not be afraid of being and acting up to the point of folly for the love of God.

It is true that you, as a sinner, wound the heart of Jesus, but it is also true that He wants you to remain in His heart.

May your meditations
and the resolutions that you make
be converted into your master plan of life,
the life long plan of your way to sanctity.

The meditation introduces you into a specific and determined reality of your life – you will be learning to enter into continuous dialogue with God. Day after day you will be discovering newer and deeper contents of the Divine truths. These, through the graces that will be conceded to you,

> will bring you closer to God,
> will transform you,
> will lead you to a life of faith
> and to the realization of that which is growing in your interior life thanks to these graces.

God entrusts His treasures to your hands, with the intent that you will choose to live by them; with the aim of living by these great treasures and having consciousness of His love, they may be converted into your hope and your joy.

CHAPTER 4

MEDITATION BASED ON THE LORD'S PRAYER

The principal part of meditation is the **adoration of God**:
that is, to remain before the presence of God in
the attitude of adoration
and meditating on what He wants to communicate to you –
whether it be through the word that you read
or through specific interior experiences.

It may happen that you may not be able to concentrate on
the words, but rather on your experience of misery and on the
love of God that is always favorable toward you.

"OUR FATHER"

When, in the spirit of faith, you become aware
that you are before the presence of your Heavenly Father
face to face,
remain before Him **with childlike trust**.

Jesus taught this to the Apostles
when He told them
that they could address God with the words: "Our Father"
(Mt 6:9).

In this way, adore Him who is always with you
in the attitude of admitting your nothingness,
and at the same time, with childlike trust before God.

This kind of adoration can lead you to a genuine fear of God. During the moment of the Annunciation, when Mary found herself face-to-face with the presence of God, "she was greatly troubled" (Lk 1:29). But then "the angel said to her, 'Do not be afraid, Mary'" (Lk 1:30).

God waits so that when He is revealed to you during prayer,
your response would be that of adoration,
in the attitude of childlike trust.

"YOUR KINGDOM COME"

If you want to continue your meditation,
you can reflect on the following words of the Lord's Prayer:
May "your kingdom come" (Mt 6:10).

This stage of meditation will deepen your consciousness that, as a child of God, you are called to construct the Reign of God on earth.

Then, express your joy to the Creator
for receiving the unfathomable gift of being
an 'adopted child' (cf. Rom 8:15).
At the same time,

by standing in the truth before God,
show to Him your empty hands.

This is one form of communion with God, of uniting yourself more with Him through the knowledge of that great dignity to which you have been elevated. It can be realized either through the reflection based on the text, or through the interior experience of your own misery and God's boundless love for you.

In showing to God your empty hands and the truth that in the construction of His Kingdom you are a useless servant, it must be accompanied always by a bold trust in God's mercy and forgiveness. God expects that you trust that **His love infinitely surpasses your indignity.**

At the Annunciation, when the angel revealed to Mary God's plans, she experienced her lowliness, but it did not diminish her faith in God's love.

"YOUR WILL BE DONE"

In the following stage
the meditation of the words, "your will be done" (Mt 6:10),
can deepen your desire of fulfilling the will of God.

The process of knowing the love of God leads to a more intensified desire to be docile to His will in everything.

The Most Blessed Virgin Mary said, "'may it be done,'" in response to the limitless love shown her at the Annunciation. And so it should be in your life, as well. When, in the course of your meditation, God reveals His love for you, be it through the words of the text or through the interior experience of certain truths, your most appropriate response should be the desire to totally submit yourself to Him.

Mary expressed her desire of fulfilling the will of God with the words: "'Behold, I am the handmaid of the Lord. May it be done to me according to your word'" (Lk 1:38). You too, should say to God:

> Father, You know how miserable I am;
> You know that if I am my own guide, I will be lost;
> because of this, permit me to be Your servant-slave.
> Adequately responding to that which You reveal to me
> > surpasses me completely.
> Thus, I want to submit myself to You in every moment of
> my life.
> Even when — as a slave —
> I may not fully understand Your way of acting,
> I want to accept everything, whatever You may send me.
> I want to recognize that this is the best for me,
> not by obligation,
> but because in the deepest part of my heart
> I desire to fulfill only Your will,
> even when I cannot understand it.

This form of ending the meditation can be used at various stages of interior life. We can utilize this method, as when we fill the vessel of our soul with the aid of our reason, memory and affections, or at more advanced levels, when we can no longer find support in discursive meditation.[11] In this case, the

---

[11] Discursive prayer: "That form of prayer in which the reflections of the mind are more active than the affections of the will. It is called discursive because discursion is the act of the mind that proceeds from one truth to the knowledge of another truth, either about the same object or about something else." *Modern Catholic Dictionary*, s.v. "discursive prayer."

meditation is converted in a state of remaining in the presence of God, and in being focused in some general idea. This **prayer of recollection**[12] (according to the definition of St. Teresa of Avila) consists in the faculties of the soul being concentrated on God intuitively, in order to receive everything that He wants to communicate to us, in order to surrender totally to His actions and, as a consequence, to fulfill His will in everything.

---

[12] The prayer of recollection, according to St. Teresa of Avila, is the living awareness that God is in us. It is the second degree of prayer (the first is the meditation). It consists in assuming an active consciousness. This signifies that the work effort of intellect as well as of the will, like the gaze of faith, play an important role. The soul itself tries to take consciousness of the presence of God in itself. This prayer consists in breaking away from the creatures and in starting the communication with God through the gaze of faith. It is not treated here only as taking consciousness of the presence of God that sustains the existence, because this is reason enough. It involves the presence of God that is an exclusive object of faith: the presence of God that comes to us, is entrusted to us so that we may know Him, we may love Him, and in a certain degree we may feel the joy through His presence already here on earth. However, this "enjoying" of God's presence, is already, to a certain degree, a passive thing that the soul cannot create by itself, but flows from the gift of the Holy Spirit. The faith mentioned above is sufficient to start an intimate and filial communication with God. This prayer is a certain, but blurred, knowledge. The prayer of recollection can be said at the same level of any form of prayer.

St. Teresa indicates three advantages of the prayer of recollection. The soul acquires a certain dominion over its senses. The love of God burns with more facility (easiness) in the soul. The prayer of recollection prepares the soul for the infused prayer (for the prayer of quiet and for the unifying prayer).

By ourselves, we can reach the level of prayer of recollection. St. Teresa assures us that with persevering work, with the help of God, the prayer of recollection can be attained in one year or even half a year. There are three means that help to attain this objective:

— To imagine God by ourselves in prayer with the help of some image, because even though we cannot feel it when we want, we can imagine God by ourselves when we desire it.

— To totally entrust oneself to the Lord, to offer our will to the will of God, letting ourselves be attracted by Him, because He defines our consent.

— To take consciousness of His presence during the whole day; doing all occupations with Him.

Cf. Gabriele di Santa Maria Maddalena, *La via dell'orazione* (The Path of Prayer) (Rome: n.p., 1955), 157-168.

Through this form of meditation, God can eventually lead you to the **prayer of quiet**.[13]

Try to benefit from the help of your confessor in choosing the methods and forms of meditation, so that in every stage of interior life you can totally submit yourself to the action of the Holy Spirit.

This action of the Holy Spirit will intensify

in the measure by which you call on Him

with the awareness of your spiritual misery.

You, a sinner, badly need His saving and healing power.

Then you will discover **in meditation** how important it is to have

the attitude of the tax collector.

---

[13] The prayer of quiet is a supernatural prayer; that is to say, we cannot acquire it by ourselves. By our extreme misery, we are not capable of celebrating, praising, adoring, nor extolling God worthily. For this, He Himself comes to help our weakness, giving us already here on earth the foretaste of participation in His Kingdom.

This is the third level of prayer. It encompasses the initial part of pure contemplation, when the soul is no longer served by the imagination nor concepts, but only the love and "sense of God" reign in the soul. It is a passive prayer not in the sense that it excludes our activity, but because by ourselves we cannot attain it by our own initiative. The prayer of quiet is realized under the influence of the gifts of the Holy Spirit, in which it depends exclusively on God. We can only prepare ourselves for it. This state of prayer can be presented in different grades, according to every soul, until the unifying level, which is the prayer of quiet in a very strong intensity. With His presence, the Lord introduces the soul to a state of profound peace. All of its faculties are silenced; it perceives God neither with the imagination, nor with sentiments. It is a knowledge that flows from within; it is a knowledge of love. The supernatural love is a friendship, a mutual benevolence. We desire Him, the good of the Lord, but He desires the good for us much more and for this He attracts us to Him. The reason does not create new concepts, but it awakens in us the "sense of God," in order to orient our life toward Him. The soul comprehends to what degree God, who embraces the soul, is truly unique, incomparably majestic and superior to all.

The soul's experience is like a suspension of all its faculties (interior and exterior); even the body experiences a sweet peace. The will, attracted to God, is so happy that it would no longer want to retrieve its freedom, for it cannot be separated from the Lord. One's faculty of reason can be distracted and bring the soul along on its wandering, disturbing the peace of the will. The memory helps the soul in this work and the soul can yield to the distraction from its loving attention in which the will is submerged. However, if the Lord attracts the soul more profoundly, then the influence over reason will be so strong that the reason also will obtain peace.

The prayer of quiet can be realized during the time destined to prayer, and it can continue and be prolonged throughout the day. The will can be united to God during the realization of ordinary activities. St. Teresa says that the prayer of quiet is the first supernatural prayer and everybody should reach this level, even though not all arrive at the unitive prayer. Cf. Gabriele di Santa Maria Maddalena, *La via dell'orazione*, 169-181.

PART TWO

GOD IS IN LOVE WITH YOU

To believe means to 'entrust' ourselves, like the sheep in the Gospel entrusts itself with all its limitations, frailty, and weakness to the One who reveals Himself as the Good Shepherd. He loves without limit, and calls His sheep, inviting them to remain in His outstretched arms in a loving embrace.

John Paul II says:

To believe is to 'entrust' this *human 'I'*, in all its transcendence and all its transcendent greatness, but also with its limits, its fragility and its mortal condition, to *Someone* who announces himself as the *beginning* and the *end*, transcending all that is created and contingent, but who also reveals himself at the same time as a Person who invites us to companionship, participation and 'communion'.[14]

---

[14] A. Frossard, *"Be Not Afraid!"*, 64-65. Single quotation marks added by author.

CHAPTER 5

"THEY WERE LIKE SHEEP WITHOUT A SHEPHERD" (MK 6:34)

Those who recognize their own weakness and helplessness
and trustfully await everything from God
are likened to, in the Gospel, the "sheep without a shepherd."
The relationship of Jesus to such persons is very special –
since going out of His way in meeting their expectations,
the Good Shepherd is disposed to make for them
an additional effort,
and even to perform miracles.

St. Mark describes it in this way: "The apostles gathered together with Jesus and reported all they had done and taught. He said to them, 'Come away by yourselves to a deserted place and rest a while.' People were coming and going in great numbers, and they had no opportunity even to eat. So they went off in the boat by themselves to a deserted place. People saw them leaving and many came to know about it. They hastened there on foot from all the towns and arrived at the place before them. When he disembarked and saw the vast crowd, his heart was moved with pity for them, for they were like sheep without a shepherd; and he began to teach them many things" (Mk 6:30-34).

How surprising it is! Jesus beforehand had clearly expressed His will: ". . . 'Come away by yourselves to a deserted place and rest a while'," and then He changed a decision which He had already made! Here, the attitude of His listeners was decisive: "... his heart was moved with pity for them, for *they were like sheep without a shepherd*."

WITHOUT YOU I WILL PERISH

> The attitude of the **sheep without a shepherd**
> must be something special before God's eyes;
> it is the attitude of recognizing one's own incapacity
> and weakness,
> the inability to live without the Shepherd.

Imagine a newly born lamb that can hardly stand on its wobbly legs, with its huge eyes looking at the shepherd, as if telling him:

> You know how weak and invalid I am;
> you know that without your help I will be lost;
> that without you I will perish.

Perhaps Christ noticed something of this attitude in the conduct of the people for whom it was very difficult to be separated from Him. Seeing Him take the boat, they followed Him. Before the arrival of Jesus on the other side of the lake, "they hastened there on foot." There must have been something extraordinary in their attitude, since Jesus renounced His own plans – because He saw:

> how very thirsty they were for
> His words and
> His presence.
> It is necessary that you also should know your own weakness,
> that you may accept the fact that without Jesus you will perish,
> that you cannot live without Him.

The attitude of the **sheep without a shepherd** does not mean passivity; on the contrary, it is an attitude full of dynamism. They were listening to Jesus, as St. Mark writes. They were very active. In fact, it was not easy to walk or, perhaps, to run along the coastline and to arrive before Jesus and the Apostles who traveled by boat. They undertook this effort without assurance that Jesus would still want to remain with them. They were certainly not expecting new miracles, either. Nevertheless, they desired to be near Him.

The sheep without a shepherd **is persistently searching** for Him. It is the contrary attitude of the **lost sheep**, who being unfaithful to the will of the shepherd, and in a conscious and voluntary manner, separates itself from the shepherd.

> You are the sheep who searches for the shepherd
> – when in times of spiritual dryness and darkness, you
> try to pray, even though you do not feel the presence of God

– when you stretch out your hands in darkness, and
through faith you try meeting and 'touching' God
who is hidden in darkness.

In these moments you will experience your spiritual weakness and
you will better understand that you need help. Therefore, Jesus
will throw His 'pearls' before you,
even though previously
He would not have had the intention of doing so.

In response to the attitude of those who were
listening to Him,
He not only changed His decision
but even performed a miracle –
the great miracle of multiplication of bread,
an anticipation of the institution of the Eucharist,
the miraculous presence
of the Living Bread
in the Church.

Thanks to the attitude of the **sheep without a shepherd**,
an attitude that 'captivates God',
He will realize great miracles in your life.
He will grant you His special graces.

God will even give you the most precious evangelical 'pearls'.

THE TRIAL OF FAITH WHICH PRECEDES
THE MIRACLE

Before performing the miracle of the loaves, Jesus put the
Apostles through a trial of faith – a very difficult one.

First, He tells them that they can rest and eat. After many hours of continual service, they are very tired, but in spite of this, the Master continues teaching for many hours. Then, when the Apostles were more tired and hungry, He indicates to them: "'Give them some food yourselves'" (Mk 6:37).

God expresses His will. He tells them that He wants **them** to give something to eat to the multitude of people. This appears to be completely impossible since they were in the desert and they did not have provisions for them. They find that they have only five loaves of bread and two fish (cf. Mk 6:38). Nevertheless, this time Christ does not alter His decision.

Christ puts the Apostles in a situation in which it is not possible to have support either from their human reason or from experience – until then they have not been witnesses of any miracle of the multiplication of loaves.

Neither were their feelings a support for them: it is very difficult to have positive feelings when one is hungry and tired and then things completely impossible, illogical, and even absurd are demanded of you.

Precisely when the Apostles found themselves in these conditions, they were put into a difficult trial of faith.

OBEDIENT IN SPITE OF EVERYTHING

The attitude of the Apostles at this moment must have been similar to **the attitude of the helpless sheep,** which in experiencing their own weakness, await everything from the shepherd. This situation, in some manner, obliged them to it. Undoubtedly because of this,

> with living faith, they looked at Jesus,
> the Divine Shepherd,
> and contrary to their experiences,
> to their feelings,
> and against reason,
> they obeyed Him.

When Jesus instructed them to divide the multitude into small groups and tell the people to be seated on the grass, the Apostles undoubtedly feared being discredited. There could have been an interior conflict for them. By instructing the people in such a way, they knew that they would take it as an invitation to eat. In fact, such a suggestion is not made if there is no food to offer them. Nonetheless, without considering their own feelings, they followed the instructions of Jesus.

> A person who has the attitude of the sheep who recognizes
> > its own helplessness,
> searches for the Divine Shepherd
> and when he encounters Him,
> he shows Him his total trust,
> and listens to His voice in everything.
> The Apostles behaved in such a way.
> They were obedient
> contrary to their experience,
> feelings,
> and reason.

And then, in response to this obedience of faith, God performs a miracle: "Then, taking the five loaves and the two fish and looking up to heaven, he said the blessing, broke the loaves, and gave them to [his] disciples to set before the people; he also divided the two fish among them all (Mk 6:41).

GOD WANTS TO BE 'CAPTIVATED' BY YOUR HUMILITY

The act of breaking bread, that special sign of love, was an annunciation of the Blessed Sacrament instituted by Jesus on Holy Thursday.

> When you know better your own weakness
> and agree to such truth,
> that you are incapable of living
> without Jesus
> the Good Shepherd,
> you will be able to discover
> to a greater depth the mystery of the Eucharist.

Through this first miracle of the multiplication of the loaves, Jesus tells you:

> Be like those who listen to Me,
> and you will even receive the graces
> > that of yourself, you are not capable
> > of imagining.
> > You can attract Me to perform miracles, even
> > the greatest.
> With such an attitude, you 'captivate' Me
> and I want to be 'captivated' by you

within such an attitude.

The attitude of the sheep without the shepherd opens the treasury of the Divine Mercy. Thanks to this attitude, God can give you more valuable graces –

you will receive the 'pearls'
that will enable you to fully benefit from the Holy Mass,
the Holy Eucharist,
the Sacrament of Reconciliation,
the adoration of the Most Blessed Sacrament
and prayer.

WHEN THE SHEEP 'TURNS' INTO A PIG

The attitude of the helpless and invalid sheep is not stable in our life. On the contrary, to remain in it demands a special interior vigilance. It is paradoxical – when you are gifted with more valuable pearls, at the same time you are in great danger! Because you are confronted with the temptation of pride, it is very easy to succumb.

Exactly that happened to those who were listening to Jesus. They were so self-assured that after the miracle of the multiplication of the loaves, they tried to 'manipulate' God – they resolved to take Jesus by force. As St. John describes it: "When the people saw the sign he had done, they said, 'This is truly the Prophet, the one who is to come into the world.' Since Jesus knew that they were going to come and carry him off to make him king, he withdrew again to the mountain alone" (Jn 6:14-15).

Immediately they closed themselves to God!

There must have been an enormous pride that was born in them –
> they wanted to take Jesus by force,
> to capture Him against His will.

Without noticing it, they passed from the attitude of the sheep without a shepherd to the attitude of the proud evangelical pigs
> which trample the valuable pearls;
> who, filled with pride and disregarding everyone,
> want to impose their own will
> on the Good Shepherd.

At the beginning they were so open to Jesus, they really needed Him so much. When they witnessed the miracle of the multiplication of the loaves, they knew that Jesus could remedy all their needs, and they abandoned the attitude akin to the weak and helpless sheep. They felt strong and they became proud.

For this, the Good Shepherd distanced Himself from them.

In the Sermon on the Mount, Christ says do not throw pearls in front of pigs (cf. Mt 7:6). While we possess the attitude of the evangelical pigs which are proud, we are pleased with ourselves and concerned with self-contentment. We will be closed to the presence of God in us. In this situation, we are not capable either of recognizing or even receiving the most valuable 'pearls'.

> Therefore, we do not benefit fully from Holy Mass,
> > Holy Eucharist,
> > confession,
> > adoration or meditation,
> > or indeed from a spiritual conference,

since the attitude of the evangelical pigs
closes us to grace.

Try to remain in the attitude of the helpless sheep, otherwise, when God would give you His most precious gifts in a special way, you will consider that the 'pearls' received are yours. And by attributing and appropriating the gifts of God to yourself, you convert yourself into the attitude of the evangelical pigs.

And so the attitude of the sheep without the shepherd should become the master plan of your entire life.

WHEN WE RELY ON OURSELVES

A similar situation occurred in the case of the Apostles. There was a similar change in their attitude: Jesus "made his disciples get into the boat and precede him to the other side toward Bethsaida, while he dismissed the crowd. And when he had taken leave of them, he went off to the mountain to pray. When it was evening, the boat was far out on the sea and he was alone on shore. Then he saw that they were tossed about while rowing, for the wind was against them. About the fourth watch of the night, he came toward them walking on the sea. He meant to pass by them. But when they saw him walking on the sea, they thought it was a ghost and cried out. They had all seen him and were terrified. But at once he spoke with them, 'Take courage, it is I, do not be afraid!' He got into the boat with them and the wind died down. They were [completely] astounded. They had not understood the incident of the loaves. On the contrary, their hearts were hardened" (Mk 6:45-52).

The Apostles, so open and obedient before the miracle of the loaves, afterwards closed themselves to Jesus. By struggling against the wind and the waves, they tried to overcome the difficulties by themselves; they wanted to overcome the waves hurled against them through their own forces. They no longer had the attitude of the helpless sheep, as they did when Jesus told them: "'Give them some food yourselves.'"

During that moment, they were awaiting everything from God.
But now they depended only on themselves.

If they would have had the attitude of helplessness and trust, Jesus, who undoubtedly wanted to help them, immediately could have appeared and could have calmed the heavy waves.

But Jesus "meant to pass by them."
Why?
Perhaps the attitude of the evangelical pigs
was already present within them (cf. Mt 7:6)
that they no longer needed God,
because they wanted to be god for themselves.

The Apostles then despised the miracle of the multiplication of the loaves: "They had not understood the incident of the loaves. On the contrary, their hearts were hardened." They also despised the grace of the attitude of the sheep without a shepherd, which had been granted to them.

Certainly they were prone to rely above everything else
on themselves,
and, consequently, it was very difficult to have the recognition
of one's own weakness and helplessness.

However, Jesus did not abandon His Apostles to their own forces. He wanted to help them so that they might consider their inappropriate and incorrect attitude. That is why – walking near the boat, wanting to pass them by – He makes Himself visible to them.

EVEN THOUGH IT BE ONLY A FEEBLE
AND MISERABLE CALL

"But when they saw him walking on the sea, they thought it was a ghost and cried out. They had all seen him and were terrified"(Mk 6:49-50).

The disciples began to be afraid. This was probably not fear of God but simply a human fear. However, in the midst of this human confusion and fear, they began to call on Jesus.

Thus, something had changed in their attitudes.
As a response, Jesus immediately appeared in their boat
to help them:
because they called upon Him.

Although it was only a miserable and feeble call, full of fright, caused principally by human fear, Jesus responded: "He got into the boat with them and the wind died down"(Mk 6:51).

It is not enough that only in the most difficult situations in life
you stand before God with the attitude of the sheep without
a shepherd.
It is necessary that **at all times** you recognize your own weakness
and the truth of your nothingness,
that you remember **always**

70

that you will perish
if you do not trust in the Good Shepherd.
Only when you remain
continuously in the attitude
of the *sheep without a shepherd,*
weak and sinful as you are,
will God enable you to benefit
    from His most precious graces,
especially from the graces of the Eucharist
and the Sacrament of Reconciliation.
And they will **transform** you.

CHAPTER 6

THE HELPLESSNESS OF THE SHEEP WITHOUT A SHEPHERD

A special characteristic of the sheep without a shepherd is its helplessness.

Imagine for yourself a flock of sheep following in the steps of the shepherd. Amongst them, somewhere at the end, **the last among the sheep** is limping and dragging its feet slowly along with much difficulty. The rest are running behind the shepherd, but this one, even though it wants to be obedient, always finds itself to be last. When the shepherd calls the sheep, those that are obedient and faithful run rapidly to him and they are very near him. The last sheep, which also has good will, continuously remains the last, far from the shepherd. It has no strength and nothing works out well for it. Limping and falling, it can only try to follow the shepherd.

THE ONE WHOSE HELPLESSNESS BECOMES EXTREME

Perhaps this sheep that limps, falls many times on the ground and drags its feet along the way is a familiar image to you. You know it through your own experience. Perhaps it remains difficult for you to affirm that you run and walk close behind Christ. Perhaps you sense yourself more as someone that drags himself along or merely desires to drag himself along.

You are like **the sheep without a shepherd – the helpless sheep.**
The weak and helpless sheep
arrives much later than the others at the meeting place with Jesus.
But in fact it arrives!
And it receives a great prize: it is near the Divine Shepherd,
and who knows, it may even be the one who is nearest.

The helpless sheep wants to follow Jesus,
even though nothing works out well for it
and the efforts that it makes do not have results.
It believes that the Good Shepherd sees its desire to follow Him,
and its effort to advance at least by a few steps.
It believes that in the eyes of the Good Shepherd it is not important
how much distance it has successfully taken
but only the extent and greatness of its desire and effort
to be obedient to Him.

But what happens if this sheep, which drags itself along, doubts that the Good Shepherd loves and waits for him? Then, something terrible occurs:

it remains immobile and 'contemplates' its incapacity.

It withdraws to itself and, unconsoled, remains in sadness
and despair.
However, this sadness and suffering are its own fault.
To remain in sadness is never an appropriate attitude.
After all, the Good Shepherd is waiting for you.
So, then, why do you linger and detain yourself?
It doesn't matter and is not important
that the others may go ahead of you:
that they may be already near the Shepherd.
It does not matter that from a human point of view
there may be no hope that someday you will be near Him.
Do not allow yourself to be guided too much by your own reason.
You must begin to let yourself be guided by God's logic.
Only He knows the value of the 'limping steps' of the sheep that
drags itself along.

FOLLOWING IN THE STEPS OF THE ONE WHO IS AN ABYSS OF HELPLESSNESS AND TRUSTFULNESS

If you want to walk toward God along the path of the helpless
sheep, you do not have to force yourself to be like the **eagles**.[15] By
adopting the attitude of the helpless sheep, you too can imitate
the highest model of sanctity – the One whose only desire was to
be the servant – slave of the Lord.

The Most Blessed Virgin lived the attitude of the helpless
sheep in a most perfect manner. It was she who knew best that

---

[15] St. Thérèse of Lisieux, *Story of a Soul: The Autobiography of St Thérèse of Lisieux*, 3rd ed., trans. John Clarke, O.C.D. (Washington, DC: ICS Publications, 1996), 199.

without God, nothing is possible. She was, in her own "yes," like an abyss[7] of **helplessness and poverty**, and at the same time an **abyss of trust in God**.

When you begin to imitate Mary – by recognizing your weakness and yearning trustfully to see the Good Shepherd, who is invisible to you – you will be able to follow Him with perseverance and live with the hope that He will take care of you, even if you are the last.

This attitude attracts Christ.

And so, then, following the example of Mary,
> when you begin to be an abyss of incapacity
> as well as trustfulness,
> God will fill you
> with the abyss of His Divine mercy,
> because "deep calls to deep" (Ps 42:8).

TO LIVE THE PRAYER OF THE HELPLESS SHEEP

The attitude of the *helpless sheep* will not become permanent in your life without prayer – without the prayer of the *helpless sheep*.
> Desiring to live this form of prayer,
> try to put yourself trustfully before God
> with the awareness of your frailty
> or even your total weakness:
> *Lord,*
> *here I am last, dragging myself along,*
> *because I am the worst.*
> *Nevertheless, I believe*
> *that You are waiting for me*

and You love me.
Lord,
I will die
if You abandon me,
if You do not take me in Your arms.
Without You I am a useless instrument,
without You I cannot live.

This prayer need not be accompanied by the feeling that Jesus takes you into His arms or the awareness of being like a helpless sheep gifted with the 'pearls' of special graces. Even if this may happen, it is better that He would hide these things from you, so that you will not appropriate to yourself the 'pearls' given you.

Ideally, in praying, you would neither feel
    your own poverty nor helplessness.
When you find yourself in this emptiness,
without feelings, without even knowing whether God is present or not,
wanting only to believe
that you are before Someone who loves you,
even though the word 'loves' may seem to you strangely empty,
then will that transformation of your interior life
begin to be realized.

However, it is important that the attitude of humility be formed in you.

Do not think that as you remain before God in interior emptiness,
He will fill you with Himself with total certainty.
It is not possible 'to manipulate' God.
God is not obliged to descend on you in such a special way.

And if He does so,
be vigilant of not appropriating it to yourself.
You could feel like the strong sheep,
which He would have to abandon.

Try to begin the day with the prayer of the *helpless sheep*:
kneel before the Lord and in the presence of the Crucified Jesus,
or before another of His images, pray with the prayer of empty
hands or with a focused gaze directed at the Cross. Remain in the
presence of Jesus with the attitude of the **helpless sheep**. This
prayer should accompany you throughout your whole day.

However, you must remember that in order to
respond to the call of Christ:
"Watch and pray" (Mk 14:38),
you cannot rely on your own strength;
otherwise, instead of praying, you will sleep,
like the Apostles in the garden of Gethsemane.

You are the last one, dragging yourself – your prayer is so poor,
you are accompanying Jesus in such a miserable manner.
It does not matter!
It is critical that you **put your hope totally in Him,**
when in response to your attitude, God fills you with His presence,
then,
according to how you remain in the attitude of the **helpless sheep**,
you await everything from Him.
He Himself can live in you and act through you.
Thanks to the attitude of the *helpless sheep*, you can continuously
discover more fully
your weakness,
your poverty,

and your spiritual misery.

You can also discover more fully the truth that God really loves the sinner in a special way,

and the truth about the lost sheep whom the Shepherd carries on His shoulders.

CHAPTER 7

THE LOST SHEEP
ON THE SHEPHERD'S
SHOULDERS

The call to union with God
always exceeds us.
It is the call to live in the truth
and to abandon
oneself
to God.
The appropriate response consists in recognizing
one's own sinfulness,
helplessness,
and weakness,
but above all
in **trusting in the Merciful Love of God.**

We conquer the heart of the Good Shepherd only with our trustful abandonment to Him.

The process of knowing our frailty and our spiritual misery can generate discouragement in us. In order to overcome it, it is useful to meditate on the message contained in the parable of the lost sheep: "The tax collectors and sinners were all drawing near to listen to him, but the Pharisees and scribes began to complain, saying, 'This man welcomes sinners and eats with them.' So to them he addressed this parable. 'What man among you having a hundred sheep and losing one of them would not leave the ninety-nine in the desert and go after the lost one until he finds it? And when he does find it, he sets it on his shoulders with great joy and, upon his arrival home, he calls together his friends and neighbors and says to them, 'Rejoice with me because I have found my lost sheep.' I tell you, in just the same way there will be more joy in heaven over one sinner who repents than over ninety-nine righteous people who have no need of repentance" (Lk 15:1-7).

NOW GOD LOVES YOU MORE THAN BEFORE THE FALL

Depression, sadness, or distrust always dominate us after sinning, and even without sinning, when in a given moment we become aware that we are great sinners. These feelings, by influencing our will to a certain degree, detain decisively the growth of interior life. They are expressions of lack of faith and lack of attitude of abandonment.

The sadness in the sphere of the will is also a sign of
lack of gratitude to God for His graces.

And an ungrateful heart closes oneself to God.
He wants to continuously give you gifts,
but ungratefulness is a kind of barrier between you and God.

When you sin
or you are saddened,
you do not trust God
and you are not grateful,
you are making yourself similar to the *lost sheep*.

What does the Good Shepherd do then?

In response to your infidelity
He searches for you,
and immediately when you show contrition,
He takes you in His arms,
showing you this gesture, that He pardoned you already.
He wants you to know
that He loves you constantly,
even

m o r e
than before your fall.
That is when He loves you more than ever.

When the father shows his welcome to the prodigal son, he says: "Quickly bring the finest robe and put it on him" (Lk 15:22). The prodigal son recognizes his sin, and as a response, the good father orders that they bring him **the best** robe. That son who returns receives the **maximum.**

It is the same expression as the Good Shepherd when he takes the lost sheep over His shoulders.

St. Thérèse of the Child Jesus says that after confessing our sins to God, ". . . He will love us even more tenderly than before we fell."[16]

And so, do not yield to the **temptation** of sadness
caused by the evil that you see in your life.
Contrition and **faith** in God's love are more important.
God *wants* to forgive.
His greatest desire is to greatly manifest His merciful love to us.
If you are a sinner who is converted,
you have a special right to this love of His –
extraordinary love
that expresses itself
and is constantly inclined to the abyss of your frailty
and of your nothingness.

THE SOURCE OF FORGIVENESS

You must remember where the source of God's boundless
forgiveness is.
Remember that
in order to give you the right to it
and to bestow on you His maximum love and tenderness,
God dies in His Son on the Cross for you.
He gives Himself to you.

This is a great mystery, the mystery of God's love, the sign of which is the **Cross**. Our right to the forgiving love of God flows from the redemptive sacrifice of Jesus on the Cross.

---

[16] St. Thérèse of Lisieux, St. *Thérèse of Lisieux: The Little Flower of Jesus*, trans. Rev. Thomas N. Taylor (London: Burns Oates & Washbourne LTD., 1944), 310.

You cannot forget
that Jesus who carries you in His arms and embraces you
bears the marks of the wounds that you inflict on Him.
That His head crowned with thorns is bloody,
His nailed feet and hands are bleeding,
His heart pierced by a lance is oozing with blood.

Every Holy Mass reminds you about it,
when the redeeming sacrifice of Him who suffers for you is made
present.

Rejoice, then, because of the forgiveness of Jesus.

However, you should not fall to the other extreme, which
consists of taking your sins lightly. This is a kind of wickedness
and applies not only to grave sins but also to venial sins and
imperfections.

Even if you wound God extremely and commit a mortal sin,
your contrition is sufficient enough for the Good Shepherd to
'carry you on his shoulders'. After asking for His forgiveness, you
must have recourse to the Sacrament of Reconciliation as soon as
possible. In response to your contrition and faith in His love,
Christ will give His forgiveness through the ministry of His priest.
If for some objective reasons the Sacrament of Reconciliation is
unavailable for you, He will conditionally pardon you for your
repentance and your trust in His mercy.

When you understand better the meaning of the parable of the
lost sheep,
perfect contrition
can be a reality in your interior life.
Then you will no longer repent out of fear of punishment,

but because your sin and infidelity
have wounded God.
You will repent because you have betrayed Someone who
desires
                to live in your heart,
who constantly bestows upon you His unique love –
His forgiving love.
This kind of contrition will purify you from your faults.

Grace is necessary for this to be possible. However, trust is
needed that God may give His grace when the sinner is repentant
for scorning the Good Shepherd's love. In this moment, perfect
contrition may appear in the soul to a certain degree.

Only in the future life will you know
the whole depth of the mystery of God's love that pardons,
and whose sign is the **Cross**.
However, here on earth,
this mystery will accompany you at every stage of your interior life.

In the midst of great darkness
the Cross
will always be for you
a **shining source of light**
to which you can continually have recourse.
This will be your return to the Source
from which springs your right to be forgiven.

Another form of closing ourselves to God's pardon can be
remaining in sadness, in discouragement, and in distrust.
To succumb to these feelings is an expression of lack of trust.

Your greatest tragedy could be that you would not want to receive forgiveness from God and, consequently, your rejection of such grace.

GOD WANTS THE CONSEQUENCES OF EVIL

The parable of the lost sheep also explains the following:
God does not want the sin,
because ours sins 'nailed' His Son to the Cross.
However, He wants the consequences of sin:
contrition for the committed evil
and our discovery of His forgiving love.
Through His forgiveness,
God wants to bestow upon us *His maximum love* –
and so, if the offense against God does not bring contrition
and discovery of His love, it would be necessary to commit
sins as frequently as possible, in order to be carried in
the arms of the Good Shepherd.

St. Thérèse of the Child Jesus expressed a similar truth when she told her sister Celine: ". . . you should be happy when you stumble and fall. . . . if in your fault there were no offence against God, you should really stumble on purpose in order to humble yourself."[17] It speaks of 'profiting' from sin by discovering **one's own misery.**[18] Sin can also help us in **discovering the depth of God's mercy.**

---

[17] Sister Genevieve of the Holy Face (Celine Martin), *A Memoir of My Sister: St. Thérèse of Lisieux*, authorized translation by the Carmelite Nuns of New York of *Conseils et Souvenirs* (New York: P.J. Kenedy & Sons, 1959), 29-30.
[18] Cf. St. Thérèse of Lisieux, *Story of a Soul: The Autobiography of St Thérèse of Lisieux*, 179.

St. Thérèse of the Child Jesus teaches us one more way to profit from sin: as an occasion to *offer to God the unpleasant consequences of our falls.* Shortly before Thérèse's death her sister Pauline (R.M. Agnes of Jesus) confided in her about the sadness and despair she felt after having committed a mistake. Thérèse answered her: "'When I commit a fault that makes me sad, I know very well that this sadness is a consequence of my infidelity, but do you believe I remain there? Oh! no, I'm not so foolish! I hasten to say to God: My God, I know I have merited this feeling of sadness, but let me offer it up to You just the same as a trial that You sent me through love. I'm sorry for my sin, but I'm happy to have this suffering to offer to You.'"[19]

> By accepting to suffer the consequences of your sins,
> try to offer that which you experience through them
> to the Good Shepherd who finds you.

YOU CANNOT LEAN ON YOURSELF

During the initial stages of interior life, feelings and understanding will accompany you as you meditate on the Gospel. In later stages, you can only know through faith the message of Christ.

For example, in meditating on the parable of the lost sheep, you can receive the message about the Good Shepherd's love in the sphere of feelings and emotions, at other times, just intellectually. However, it can also happen that you feel nothing nor understand anything, and so you can receive the words of Jesus through faith.

---

[19] St. Thérèse of Lisieux, *Her Last Conversations*, Jul. 3, no. 2, 71.

If, after each sin, you see that you are threatened by the temptation of sadness in the sphere of feelings and emotions when you ask God's forgiveness, you can try to imagine that Jesus is carrying you in His arms.

In another stage of interior life, when feelings disappear and dryness sets in, you will no longer be capable of imagining and feeling that you are carried in His arms. Then you can repeat for some time a short prayer, for example: *I thank You Jesus for carrying me in Your arms.* When you repeat these words many times, the consciousness that Jesus truly carries you in His arms can finally be awakened in your heart.

But you should not lean too much on the knowledge acquired from this form of prayer. God can also obscure your memory and your reason. In receiving the message of the Gospel, you should abandon yourself to the grace that He gives you whenever He wants.

In trying to remember after each fall that Jesus carries you in His arms when you show Him repentance, it would be a sign that you rely too much on your own memory and it would be an expression of spiritual pride. On the way to holiness, you would have to be purified from it.

God Himself will remind you about His message of love.
He will grant this grace with greater abundance,
according to the degree of your poverty in spirit.
He will grant this grace with greater abundance,
as you understand and accept with more profundity
that by yourself you are incapable

of even reminding yourself of that which He once let you understand.

WITH EYES FIXED ON THE CROSS

Try frequently to put yourself before the reality of the Cross. Then you will comprehend more deeply the mystery of God's forgiveness; it is the standard of the mystery of the redemptive sacrifice of Christ, which gives us an idea of the extent of human evil.

In adoring the Cross and
recognizing your evil,
the Crucified One embraces you toward His wounded Heart.
Try to put yourself at the foot of the Cross together with Mary
and ask her to teach you
how you must adore her Crucified Son.

Even if she was sinless, the Most Blessed Virgin Mary probably recognized her own nothingness as she stood at the foot of the Cross. Jesus 'embraced' her to His heart because of her humility. The Redemptive Sacrifice of Jesus includes Mary as well. It was by the grace of God that she was preserved from sin. It can be said that in some manner God pardoned her in anticipation of the redemptive sacrifice of Christ, preserving her from any fall. And if He pardons her, He also takes her in His arms, just as the Good Shepherd does to the lost sheep.

Mary was consciously living her own nothingness,
aware that God was constantly preserving her from sin.
The Magnificat and other fragments of the Gospel speak
about this clearly.

Because of this, she was always humble,
> trusting,
> and grateful.

In answer to this kind of attitude,
God continuously bestowed upon her His greatest love,
and she received it wholeheartedly.

SINS FROM WHICH GOD CONSTANTLY PRESERVES US

God also forgives us our sins beforehand, by preserving us from them through the power of Jesus' sacrifice. St. Thérèse of the Child Jesus said: "I know that without Him, I could have fallen as low as St. Mary Magdalene, and the profound words of Our Lord to Simon resound with a great sweetness in my soul. I know that *'he to whom less is forgiven, LOVES less,'* but I also know that Jesus *has forgiven me more* than St. *Mary Magdalene* since He forgave me *in advance* by preventing me from falling."[20]

When we are grateful for having been preserved from sin
> by the power of Christ's sacrifice,
we benefit from the special grace of the forgiving love of God.
For this, we ought to thank God,
not only because He forgives the sins committed
but also because He preserves us from many sins.
If He would not do so,
with certainty, we would have committed them.

---

[20] St. Thérèse of Lisieux, *Story of a Soul: The Autobiography of St Thérèse of Lisieux*, 83.

Without God's protection, we would commit all possible sins. In fact, Jesus says: "*without me you can do nothing*"(Jn 15:5).

It can be said that by forgiving us the sins from which we were preserved, Jesus does it with the same gesture: He takes us in His arms to show us His **greatest** love.

CHAPTER 8

TO TRUST IN THE EXAMPLE OF THE CANAANITE WOMAN

I n acknowledging our spiritual misery, we discover that instead of advancing on the way to sanctity, we stop or become aware of going in the opposite direction – the wide way toward perdition. We become a scandal for others. Only by ardently invoking God's mercy can we be preserved from sadness and discouragement.

SO SINFUL – BY BEING FULL OF ONE'S OWN VISION OF THE WORLD

According to the degree of growth in interior life, we will begin to see more clearly all the signs of our infidelities, which perhaps we previously took for granted. Even if our past sins would no longer be repeated, the feeling of dejection and discouragement

can be intensified as a result of our sinfulness. By deepening the
spiritual life, one's attention undergoes change:

> from the sins that before were easily perceived
> to those which, at the outset, are least important and
> apparently innocent.
> In reality they are like the evangelical "camel"
> (Mt 23:24).
> You will understand, for example, that your self-absorption
> and thinking in a human way are your reasons
> for saying **"no"**
> to God who has His own plans for you.

From a person who only minimally responds to the
expectations of God, who has bestowed on him a special grace,
should emerge the consciousness of great infidelity. Externally,
this kind of person can appear better than others. Nevertheless,
such a person can be aware that he deserves a long and severe
purgatory or even condemnation. He sees that he is closed to the
graces that God bestows on him and that he is focused only on
himself. He sees it and recognizes that he is one of the greatest
sinners. **WHY?** Because living according to **one's own** visions and
dreams hinders God in realizing **His** plans. And the
consequences of our impassability can be tragic because such
consequences can also be extended to many people. The evil that
can happen in this situation becomes greater in accordance to the
degree to which we do not respond to God's plan. This awareness
can be overwhelming, but at the same time can 'spur us to do
something' –

> in order that we may recognize our evil;
> in order that we may cry out to Christ with greater intensity for His
> mercy.

WHEN THE ASPIRATION TO SANCTITY APPEARS COMPLETELY UNREAL

When the awareness of your sinfulness begins to crush you heavily, faith in God's mercy can be particularly difficult for you.

The aspiration to sanctity will appear as something completely unreal to you. Strong temptations of establishing a convenient life and adhering yourself to the spirit of the world can surface. If you lack faith in God who loves you in spite of your evil, at that point you will begin to succumb to these temptations.

But, in fact, in showing you more of your sinfulness, He wants to empower you to trust even more.

If you do not benefit from such a grace, you could easily be tempted to look for a substitute to inner peace and anything or anybody that can give you a feeling of security other than God, just to calm your dejection. Then you will begin again to live according to the spirit of this world. And your egoism will 'whisper' and suggest to you:

You have to rest and take care of yourself.

You're just a human being.

Don't be so preoccupied and 'tire yourself' so much.

On the other hand, if, in experiencing your misery, you are able to trust to the point of folly, you would not direct yourself toward the pleasures of this world. You would try all the more to adhere to Christ. And you would accept the situations that make you aware that, with your evil, you belong to the worst. You would accept them as a call to trust in God's mercy without limits.

THE TRUST OF THE CANAANITE WOMAN

The Canaanite woman, presented in an extraordinarily eloquent form, teaches us the precise attitude of unlimited trust:

"And behold, a Canaanite woman of that district came and called out, 'Have pity on me, Lord, Son of David! My daughter is tormented by a demon.' But he did not say a word in answer to her" (Mt 15:22-23).

In spite of her insistent supplication, Jesus refuses to help her. However, she is not discouraged by this, and continues begging with insistence. This is how she expresses her complete trust.

A person who is proud and weak in faith will give up immediately. Such a person says to oneself:

If You are silent and do not want to do that which I ask of You,
then You consider me unworthy, and so, You reject me.
It's a waste of my time then, so I will go.
Many react in this way.
When they are put to the test,
when it appears to them that God is silent –
even if the silence of God is always apparent –
they give up
in order to look for other ways to satisfy their desire for perfect love.
But, in fact,
even when He does not respond in a visible way,
God waits so we may trust
and so we may beg Him more with greater fervor.

THE REACTION TO AN APPARENT REJECTION

The Canaanite woman begged for a spiritual grace for her daughter. The categorical refusal of Jesus could have appeared to her as His lack of mercy. If she took this situation only from the human point of view, she would definitely have been disillusioned and discouraged. But she was assessing the situation in a supernatural way.

> She responds with even more profound trust
> to the refusal of Christ.
> And with a more fervent supplication,
> she falls to her knees before Jesus and begs Him:
> She said, "Lord, help me" (Mt 15:25).

God wants to be asked.

In fact, Jesus says: "ask and you will receive" (Lk 11:9).

With her reaction, the woman confessed to Christ: I know that I am nothing but dust and that I do not deserve anything, but . . . "'Lord, help me.'" I ask You because I believe in Your omnipotence and in Your mercy.

Nevertheless, this time she again received a strong negative response: "'It is not right to take the food of the children and throw it to the dogs'" (Mt 15:26).

THE DEPTH OF HUMILITY AND FAITH

Jesus compares the Canaanite woman to the dogs as a way of verifying her humility. And she, without doubting for a single moment, accepts this 'insult'! With simplicity, she really accepts that she is not worthy, but "'even the dogs eat the scraps that fall from the table of their masters'" (Mt 15:27).

To us, proud as we are, the response of Jesus could have closed us totally to Him. We would have been disposed to 'defend our honor' at all cost. The Canaanite woman reacted in a completely different way:

> She does not claim her rights,
> but in a profound humility
> she decides to act with an unlimited trust
> that flows from an authentic recognition of her nothingness and helplessness.

"'O woman, great is your faith!'" (Mt 15:28). These words of Jesus express His admiration for this attitude. Because of this, He fulfills the petition of the Canaanite woman: "'Let it be done for you as you wish'" (Mt 15:28).

The recognition and acceptance of one's own nothingness, with childlike trust in God and faith in His love, conform to the attitude that brings about miracles.

> If it appears that God does not respond to your supplications, you have two possibilities:
> – you can be discouraged and can find consolation in what the world gives or,
> – you can perceive in God's silence an incentive to beg with greater fervor and to trust more.

Once you recognize your own unworthiness and accept the fact that you continually despise the graces that are conceded to you, you should neither lose heart nor be discouraged by the apparent absence of God's response to your supplication. While recognizing before God the truth about yourself, don't stop begging Him.

If God refuses, even in a categorical way, He does so for your salvation;

> He wants your faith to be at a point of folly
> and unlimited trust.

When you are freed from thinking in a human way, you will live your spiritual experiences, even the most difficult ones, just like the saints lived them. For example, St. Joan of Arc did not stop trusting in God even after being judged by the tribunal of a bishop. Reason could have suggested to her that she was being rejected by the Church and consequently by God. In fact, she was a very sensitive person and went through spiritual darkness.

However, she did not doubt.

CHAPTER 9

THE RETURN OF THE PRODIGAL SON

In the parable about the prodigal son, Jesus emphasizes the fullness of love that God has toward the sinner. The heavenly Father waits for our voluntary return, which is an expression of faith in His love.

"Then he said, 'A man had two sons, and the younger son said to his father, "Father, give me the share of your estate that should come to me." So the father divided the property between them. After a few days, the younger son collected all his belongings and set off to a distant country where he squandered his inheritance on a life of dissipation. When he had freely spent everything, a severe famine struck that country, and he found himself in dire need. So he hired himself out to one of the local citizens who sent him to his farm to tend the swine. And he longed to eat his fill of the pods on which the swine fed, but nobody gave him any'" (Lk 15:11-16).

THE FATHER ALLOWS THE TRAGEDY OF THE SON

To the Palestinians of those times, for someone to be employed to tend the pigs and even more, to be dying of hunger, was worse than how the pigs themselves were viewed. As to his social position, the prodigal son reached the lowest level and was regarded by people as worse than the animals, as the worst person on earth.

The father accepts his son wasting the capital that was given him, so that the son may reach the bottom of human misery, that he may be treated worse than the pigs which, for Israelites, were impure animals.

Why?

The father probably knew that his son, after receiving an enormous treasure for nothing, would not appreciate the value of the gift received. Undoubtedly, he was aware that his son would not realize that the gift was an expression of his immense fatherly love and trust. He also knew the predicament to which the treasure could lead his son since the son desired to make his own decisions and construct his happiness according to his own vision.

However, the father respected his son's will.

TO DISCOVER THE LOVE OF THE FATHER
IN FREEDOM

The evangelical father did not deprive his son of the freedom to choose, even though he foresaw a danger. However, he wanted his son to respond to his love **voluntarily**. For such to happen:

> he risked
> losing part of the estate obtained through hard work,
> the torment, the suffering,
> and even the death of his son;
> he risked
> losing his beloved son, whom he cherished deeply in his heart.

The fullness of the love of the father is expressed
in the **affirmation of the freedom** of the child
in the acceptance that his son 'could die'.
Your situation is similar.
God bestows on you priceless treasures
through the Sacrament of Baptism and the other sacraments.
He places in your hands,
according to His plans for you,
countless treasures of graces that Christ obtained for you.
In His love for you, He bestows you with an enormous capital.
At the same time, He respects your full freedom,
in order that you may discover His love
in the freedom that He gives you.

You are free. You can waste the gifts you received. But even then you have a great opportunity: by the discovery and acceptance of your own misery, you can arrive at a loving knowledge of God's profound love, and return to Him.

AT THE LOWEST ABYSS

If you become sufficiently humble,
God will enlighten you to see the extent of all your sinfulness.
He will show you that you are worse than other sinners,
even worse than the greatest sinners,
whom before you may have kept in contempt.
He will permit you to discover the most horrifying depth of
your misery.

The prodigal son, in the situation of greatest humiliation and degradation, says: "How many of my father's hired workers have more than enough food to eat, but here am I, dying from hunger" (Lk 15:17).

You also can have the impression that your soul is dying and lost when you experience the lowest depth of your spiritual misery.

You feel as if you were condemned.

You will live something like your own purgatory because it will appear to you that it is not possible that God can love someone so worthless and ungrateful, someone who wastes everything, someone who is the worst.[21] It may then be extremely difficult for you to decide to return to the Father.

You have discovered that you are the worst.

But does it mean that God no longer waits for you?

---

[21] John of the Cross *The Dark Night of the Soul* (trans. E. Allison Peers in *The Complete Works of Saint John of the Cross* vol. 1 [Westminster, MD: The Newman Press, 1990]) 2.7.7. pp. 113-115.

It is at that time that He waits for you in a special way.

It is at that point that He longs so much for your return.

When you are being tormented by the knowledge of the depth
of your misery,

the heart of the Father is burning with the greatest love for you.

If God permits that you know the truth about yourself in this degree, He does it in order to purify you from pride,

from every illusion that by yourself you are good,

and from the illusion that you are capable of
administering well

the priceless treasure you received.

And now,

after all your infidelities

and after you experienced everything **because of your own will,**

He waits,

that you may decide for a heroic act:

– being aware of the misery that is in you,

– being the worst of all . . .

you return.

SIMILAR TO THE GOOD THIEF

When the good thief was hanging on the cross beside the Redeemer, he probably was aware of the fact that he wasted everything in his life and that he was the worst. In fact, he himself recognized that he suffered justly. He saw in this suffering the consequences of his sins. In spite of this, he made a decision – a profound act of trust in Christ: "Then he said, 'Jesus, remember me when you come into your kingdom'" (Lk 23:42).

Those words reflect the attitude of the prodigal son: "'Father, I have sinned against heaven and against you. I no longer deserve to be called your son; treat me as you would treat one of your hired workers'" (Lk 15:18-19).

This is precisely the attitude that God awaits from you.

Perhaps you will know the lowest depth of your misery only at the moment of your death. And then, God will wait for the most important decision in your life: **that you want to return.**

This will save your life for all eternity.

Your incessant return after every infidelity has to prepare you for this moment. By allowing you your falls, God always desires that you grow in humility and that you discover that with His love He is inclined toward the most profound misery. Precisely as such, He prepares you for the last moment of your life – for the last trial that someday will finally arrive.

THE TRUST THAT IS LIKE OIL IN THE LAMP

It would be good if you could live with an awareness that your last trial may arrive at any time. It is necessary to be vigilant and prepared, like the wise virgins who kept oil reserves for their lamps (cf. Mt 25:1-13).

Your 'oil' should be the childlike trust in God.

From where does one get it?

That kind of trust does not have to spring from positive feelings, because it is difficult to have them when one feels his lowest.

Neither does it have to arise from the sphere of **rational** premises – when you discover the truth of your misery,

reason can tell you
that you cannot count on anything and you can expect nothing.
However, without proof from feelings, from experience, and
from logic,
your **heart**
should be filled with profound trust:
"I shall get up and go to my father" (Lk 15:18).

Thanks to this kind of **trust up to the point of folly** and the
faith that goes with it, God can bestow on you the immensity of
His graces.

What will be the best robe or sandals in your case? What
kind of ring will be put on your finger? This will remain a
mystery. But, it will be evident for you as the worst of all men that
you merit *nothing*. And so, whatever you will receive will be for you
like the best robe, the most beautiful sandals, and the most
valuable ring.

CHAPTER 10

THE PRISON – PLACE OF ENCOUNTERING LOVE

I n every circumstance of our life
God reaches out to us with His grace, with His love and
His forgiveness
in a special way – in the most painful moments.
Every situation can lead to conversion,
to a bigger openness to God
and to finding salvation in Him.

The place where sinful man experiences God's merciful love
may even be prison. After all, it is not that important under which
condition we find out that God loves us.

TO DISCOVER THE MEANING OF PAINFUL EXPERIENCES

Many prisoners receive their punishment in a totally negative way
– understood in their manner, they see it as a 'punishment from

God'. This is also true for those who have been proven guilty and sentenced justly. Why is this attitude so common? It is because our way of thinking is normally submitted to stereotypes. If according to human reasoning something is evil, then we believe that it is an objective evil. Prison, which from a human point of view is definitively an evil place, is considered also as negative in the light of faith. However, it is not absolutely the case.

In fact, there are prisoners who see their experience as a special call to change their life and to conversion. They try to see in this painful situation a sign of God's love – in fact they could have died before arriving at the prison; at the time they were committing a crime they were breaking the law and generally the commandments of God, as well. Imprisonment can be an opportunity to understand what a great evil it is to despise God's commandments.

Does it occur similarly with illness? It does. By inconveniently being bound in bed, the illness makes someone a prisoner in his own room, dependent of others because of suffering. Imprisonment as well as sickness can painfully crush, but they can also *purify*.

> They are opportunities to encounter the way toward God
> and to lovingly know His love.
>> All situations
>> in which we find out the most important truth –
>> that "God is love" (1 Jn 4:8),
>> are always **the best**.
> Do you try to find the positive dimension of difficult
> situations

of your life,
of imprisonment,
of a grave illness,
of a disabled state,
of the alcoholism of someone dear to you,
of the lack of understanding in the family?

In all the circumstances through which you pass, do you believe in the constant presence of God and in His love?

One expression of God's love can also be
that nothing goes well in your life,
that everything is complicated,
that you are frequently confused.

Discovering the meaning of all the experiences of your life is possible only through faith.

Without faith, man wants to be like God –
he wants to direct his destiny by himself alone,
he thinks that he can be happy by himself –
like God, who is the fullness of perfection and love.
He persists in the illusive conviction
that he can also be this kind of fullness.

God desires to free us and save us from this lie. Many times for this, He permits situations that **destroy our plans** and make us helpless. For someone, imprisonment can be this kind of situation. In the light of faith, this is not any different from other difficult experiences. For example, for the chosen people, the desert through which the Israelites wandered about for forty years was similar to a prison. If we try to look at the prison in the light of faith, we will understand that it is a **special place of meeting with God.**

THE PRISONER CAN BE CONVERTED INTO A GREAT SAINT

If in the light of faith everything is grace,[9] then *all* the circumstances and situations of our life are signs of God's love.

We should try to see the prison in this way as well, as a gift that is given to us. Even though it can be very difficult, we must try to see in the light of faith the supernatural dimension of suffering experienced in such a situation.

Cardinal Wyszynski,[22] who was the Primate of Poland from 1948 to 1981, strengthened and deepened his union with God in a special way when he was in prison. It was certainly a very difficult period for him, but at the same time it was a great grace. It was certainly a very important time in terms of his spiritual growth to sanctity.

Something similar happened with St. Maximilian Maria Kolbe. He would not have been a saint of such greatness if he had not been in the Nazi concentration camp of Auschwitz. It was precisely there that the process of his sanctification reached completion –

in those concrete circumstances degrading to human dignity,
of extreme humiliation, contempt, and neglect.

---

[22] Servant of God – Stefan Cardinal Wyszynski (1901-1981) directed the Church in Poland from 1948 to 1981. From 1953 to 1956 he was imprisoned by the communist authorities of the Popular Republic of Poland. Cf. Stefan Wyszynski Primate of Poland, *Letters from Prison* (Warsaw: n.p., 1990).

St. Maximilian,[23] seeing his experiences in the light of faith, accepted them as a gift. His time spent in the 'bunker', suffering with extreme hunger, was for him a time of uniting with Christ who was –

> despised,
> unjustly condemned,
> ridiculed,
> deprived of every right and dignity,
> and finally martyred and crucified
> like a thief.

The Holy Father John Paul II knows how difficult is the experience of being in prison or in the hospital. For this reason, he frequently visits the prisoners and those who are sick, asking them especially to pray[24] in a special way.

---

[23] Before being imprisoned in Auschwitz, St. Maximilian was a prisoner together with other brothers in prison camps. Brother Geronimo Wierzba describes in the following manner the vigil celebration of St. Maximilian in the prison camp of Amtitz: "He lovingly looked at us, an angelic smile adorned his face and words of gratitude flowed from his lips.... When he ended giving thanks, he continued saying: in these conditions which we find ourselves now, we accept in a special way the will of God. He takes a piece of bread, a small piece which does not suffice to anybody and ... he breaks it among the brothers.... It was a touching moment – something which is not witnessed everyday.... He spoke to us about the Immaculate, of her goodness and of her love for all of us.... She knows to convert to a greater good these circumstances which are contrary to us.... She uses us like her things and properties. May we be grateful to her because she deems it worthy to use us. Her goodness is so much in all this. They brought us here gratuitously, they gave a place to sleep and eat, so that we may win souls for her. If we would have wanted to go on a mission, how many efforts, formalities, passports would have been needed so that finally ... they would not have permitted it to us. Here we can do more good. May we take advantage of the occasion." J. Kazmeirczak, *To St. Maximilian M. Kolbe on the centenary of his birth 8-01-1994, Series: Franciscan Spirituality*, (Gdansk: n.p., 1994), 25.

[24] "That they [the sick and the suffering people] may accept that prayer may be asked from them because always with greater confidence and the greatest hope I ask prayer of those who suffer. Because through them God conquers!" From the speech that was given on June 20, 1983 at the Cathedral of Christ the King in Katowice, Poland during a pilgrimage of the Holy Father, John Paul II to Poland. Pope John Paul II, *Pokój Tobie, Polsko! Ojczyzno Moja!* (Peace Be With You, Poland! My Motherland!) (Kraków: Wydzial Duszpasterstwa Kurii Metropolitalnej, 1983), 232.

The prisoner's prayer has a great value in the eyes of the One who rejoices more "'over one sinner who repents than over ninety-nine righteous people who have no need of repentance'"(Lk 15:7). In the eyes of God, the suffering of a prisoner who is being converted has a great value. Jesus' words to the Good Thief are a testimony of this truth.

Every prisoner similar to the Good Thief can become a great saint. He does not have to be ashamed that he is in prison; it is precisely there that he comes to know God's love, and there that he is sanctified. The Good Thief is his patron. He should pray and ask from him, as he did, the grace of accepting the punishment of imprisonment, and like him grow in the love of Christ who pardons. The Good Thief recognized and accepted that the sentence given him was just. He did not rebel against such a terrible punishment. He wanted to amend the evil he committed and accepted it as necessary for his conversion.

If a prisoner who is being converted would benefit fully from the grace of being in prison, he could be sanctified rapidly.

FREEDOM IN PRISON?

When an innocent person is imprisoned, it is much more difficult for him to accept such imprisonment. This happened in one of the Latin American countries. A high-ranking and very well-respected bank executive was accused of perpetrating a great fraud and was sentenced to many years of imprisonment. Occupying an important position in the bank, this man had become so engrossed in his work that he had gone astray in his spiritual life. For him, God ceased to be of the most utmost importance.

Although he never stopped praying and always carried out his religious practices, he began to rely on himself more and more. He had a generous heart and more often helped others, but he did so at the expense of his own family. Thus, he grew in his proud self-belief that he was a good person. At work he considered himself irreplaceable. Spending more and more time at work, he neglected his wife and three children. His wife, who was heavily burdened by her obligations at home, felt the intensity of being alone and increasingly misunderstood as daily she confronted her husband's self-sufficiency and vanity. And so, his family was on the verge of breaking up. He, however, noticing none of it, went on as usual, concentrating only on his career.

Something unexpected then happened. The man was accused of having committed a serious fraud involving a large amount of money. The sum of money he was expected to repay was completely beyond his means. Thus he was sentenced to many years of imprisonment. But in fact, as to his professional honor and honesty, he had been faultless!

During the first two weeks, he was on the verge of despair. He constantly asked himself: Why me? Why has God put me in this trial? He could not understand or accept the fact that such a conscientious and responsible worker like himself should suffer many years in prison for a crime he did not commit.

But the grace of the Sacrament of Reconciliation overcame that feeling deep within him of having been unjustly accused and sentenced.

When he came into contact with a good confessor, he perceived a ray of hope for himself. He discovered the meaning of his time in prison. He understood that real **slavery** is the slavery to one's egoism and pride. There in prison, he began to regain **interior freedom**, thanks to the grace of the Sacrament of Reconciliation and the spiritual help of the confessor.

In prison he began to experience real happiness.

He said, "I am grateful to God for what had happened to me, even if it is for me to stay here in prison for the rest of my life!" He was convinced that it was necessary that God send him that trial, otherwise, being convinced of his own perfection, he would only be contented with the external manifestations of his faith.

The man was full of joy for having encountered God. With his attitude, he began to influence the other prisoners. The grace of his conversion made some of them perceive another dimension of their similar experiences.

In prison the man discovered the truth about himself. But **at the same time** he discovered the truth of the unfathomable love of God. And it was this truth that became the source of his freedom. Living in the midst of this difficult trial, he had to choose from two options:

to blame God for having allowed such an injustice,

or rather, against the dictates of pure human logic,
to believe in God's love.
He chose to believe in Love.

He did not know afterwards how his life would go on and how much time he would remain in prison.

But certainly he was already free:
through his trust in God,
through faith in His love,
and by total abandonment to Him
he obtained, most important of all,
interior freedom of heart.
And this is the most important.

For him, prison has become an authentic place of true conversion – a place of encounter of the sinner with LOVE.

PART THREE

"BEHOLD, YOUR MOTHER"

People often make reference to Christocentrism in order to contradict the devotion to Mary. It is considered as a threat to Christ, who must remain – as it is said – at the center of the religion founded in fact by Him. This demand is valid while it concerns Christ's central role in Christian life. It is not valid, however, when it deprives Jesus Christ one important dimension of His life: Jesus is the Father's Son, but He is also Mary's Son. He remains both, even in His heavenly glory. This revelation is reason enough that we may never consider Mary solely as the person who introduced her Son; solely as someone who after giving us her Son, must be forgotten thereafter in the work of redemption that her Son came to realize. Otherwise, this would cause us to forget that Jesus, being fully independent, willed to be dependent on His mother not only during the months of her pregnancy but also during the years of preparation for His public ministry. This fact alone is already more eloquent than any written text; such fact contains Marian theology. It also invites us to enter the reign of God through the privileged way of children and of those who are similar to the children (cf. Mk 10:14). Mary guarantees humility to someone who may accept to depend on God through her, in order to receive better the Spirit of her Son.[25]

---

[25] Cf. L. J. Suenens, *Mary the Mother of God*, trans. from French by a Nun of Stanbrook Abbey (New York: Hawthorne Books, 1959).

CHAPTER 11

"THE BLESSED VIRGIN ADVANCED IN HER PILGRIMAGE OF FAITH"

"While every word of Elizabeth's greeting is filled with meaning, her final words would seem to have **fundamental importance**: 'And blessed is she who believed that there would be a fulfillment of what was spoken to her from the Lord' (Lk 1:45). These words can be linked with the title 'full of grace' of the angel's greeting. Both of these texts reveal an essential Mariological content, namely the truth about Mary, who has become really present in the mystery of Christ precisely because she 'has believed.'"[26] ". . . Mary, during the pilgrimage of her filial and maternal *fiat*, 'in hope believed against hope.'"[27]

---

[26] Pope John Paul II, Encyclical Letter: *Mother of the Redeemer* (*Redemptoris Mater*) (hereafter cited as *RMat*), March 25, 1987, trans. "Vatican" (Boston, MA: Pauline Books & Media, 1987), 12.
[27] *RMat* 14.

TRIALS OF FAITH

The path to sanctity characteristically leads us through trials of faith. These are the experiences which, may be very difficult at times, because at the time of going through them we are not always able to understand the actual situation. We generally receive the grace to understand a few of these trials after they have passed. Until then, we may believe that we are in a hopeless situation.

The Israelites, who were being led to the Promised Land, experienced their trials of faith in this way. God performed miracles, but He did not solve completely all the problems of the people being led out of slavery.

> He acts similarly in your life as well.
> Even if God continuously intervenes in your life,
> He does not, however, completely resolve all of your difficulties.
> God does not free you from the call
> to accept your experiences
> **on the level of faith –**
> as in the example of the one who precedes us
> in the "pilgrimage of faith."[28]

TRIALS OF FAITH IN THE LIFE OF MARY

Mary went through especially difficult trials in her abandonment to God. Her "pilgrimage of faith" was always a constant

---

[28] Pope Paul VI, Dogmatic Constitution on the Church: *Lumen Gentium* (hereafter cited as *LG*), November 21, 1964, trans. N.C.W.C. (Boston: Pauline Books & Media, 1998), 58.

experience of new situations which surpassed all human understanding. Continuously, she offered a "full submission of intellect and will to God."[29]

The life of Mary

was an **incessant abandonment of herself to God.**

An admirable communion of persons

was realized continuously between Mary and God,

a communion built on trust,

built on an entire and continuously renewed abandonment,

and on an increasing and intensifying communion of life.

For Mary, who entrusts herself totally to God –

the will of God,

even when least comprehensible,

is the supreme value.

In living by the will of God,

she lives the life of God.

TO BELIEVE IN THAT WHICH IS HUMANLY IMPOSSIBLE

This singular relationship between God and Mary is revealed very clearly during the Annunciation, when God introduces her into an extraordinarily intimate bond with Him.

God reveals His will to her with an infinite love and Mary responds with total abandonment of herself, even if she is experiencing something that completely surpasses the capacity of human understanding. Later on, her whole life will be a constant

---

[29] Pope Paul VI, Dogmatic Constitution on Divine Revelation: *Dei Verbum* (DV), November 18, 1965, 5.

living of her *fiat* declared at the Annunciation, and at the same time, an incessant renewal of her abandonment to God.

John Paul II says that Mary teaches us the humble recognition and acceptance of the "inscrutable ways" and "unsearchable judgments" of God. "Mary, who by the eternal will of the Most High stands, one may say, at the very center of those 'inscrutable ways' and 'unsearchable judgments' of God, conforms herself to them in the dim light of faith, accepting fully and with a ready heart everything that is decreed in the divine plan."[30]

> In professing her *fiat*,
> Mary believed in something impossible,
> and later, with unwavering faith, awaited its fulfillment.
> Contrary to all rational premises, she believed in God,
> and when she was confronted with new experiences
> she invariably
> adopted only this attitude.

THE EXTRA-ORDINARY NATURE OF THE SPIRITUAL RELATIONSHIP OF JESUS AND MARY

As a response to the boundless entrustment of Mary, God bestowed on her an unimaginable grace. When Jesus was conceived, a bond between Mother and Son was born. It was not only a physical bond but also an *extraordinary spiritual bond*, whose depth will always be a great mystery for us.

---

[30] *RMat* 14.

This unrepeatable bond between Mary and God
was like a spiritual 'umbilical cord'.
Such a relationship between a creature and Creator
will never happen again.
It is because of this relationship, that St. Elizabeth,
filled with the Holy Spirit,
told Mary:
"'Most blessed are you among women'" (Lk 1:42).

When we ponder the attitude of the one who leads us in the "pilgrimage of faith," a question comes to mind: of what does the mystery of such great entrustment of Mary and of such perfect submission to the will of God consist?

In looking for the answer, we may meditate on the attitude of Mary, who leads us in the "pilgrimage of faith" and try to look at her life in the light of one of the indications of Christ: "unless you turn and become like children, you will not enter the kingdom of heaven" (Mt 18:3).

THE SPIRITUAL CHILDHOOD OF MARY

The attitude of a child is clearly seen in Mary's entrustment. At the moment of the Annunciation, being confronted with a great divine mystery, she only asked the simplest of questions among all the questions that she had the right to ask: "How can this be, since I have no relations with a man?" (Lk 1:34). Being very young, (an adolescent), it is probable that she did not have a knowledge like that of the Scribes. That is why there was such simplicity in her behavior.

She only knew that God waited for her consent –
and she accepted in such a manner.
The "yes" that she told God unhesitatingly
is a testimony that she was looking at the messenger of God
with the eyes of the evangelical child.
A child that has no vast knowledge
or experience,
does not need too many explanations –
its heart full of trust and hope, believes everything.
And Mary did not need exhaustive reasoning.

When the Incarnation was realized, she touched one of the most profound mysteries of God. She pondered such a mystery in the silence of her heart, accepting it even though it would continue to be a mystery for her.

We see this attitude of childlike trust toward God throughout her whole life, particularly during the events which were the most difficult trials of faith for her.

THE DIFFICULT SILENCE TOWARD JOSEPH

Being silent to her betrothed Joseph about the mystery of God, i.e., that "she was found with child through the holy Spirit" (Mt 1:18), must have been a very difficult trial for Mary, since she foresaw with certainty his pain and confusion.
How difficult must it have been to remain silent –
a silence about God's mystery,
as well as about her love and fidelity to Joseph.

She included in that silence the acceptance of the suffering of the one she loved, an acceptance that stemmed from the fortitude of faith.

Mary knew the Jewish law and customs. Mary also knew that conceiving a child before marriage could lead to her being stoned. "If within the city a man comes upon a maiden who is betrothed, and has relations with her, you shall bring them both out to the gate of the city and there stone them to death" (Deut 22:23-24).

The one who exemplifies for us the way of self-abandonment to God in every situation was not free from the prosaic situations in life, from the all-too-common suspicions and accusations.

The difficult experiences did not diminish her faith. God led her through them in a way known only to Him.

Moreover, she accepted every design of God.

THE ACCEPTANCE OF THE DIFFICULT EXPERIENCE IN BETHLEHEM

When Mary is directed to go to Bethlehem, she knows that the time to give birth is near. But submitting herself to the will of God, she nevertheless sets out on the long and difficult journey. She sets out with the attitude of the evangelical child and abandons herself in everything to the will of the Father, whom she loves and in whom she trusts, despite not always understanding His will.

Later, too, at the moment of the birth, she fully accepts everything that occurs and the extreme conditions, which were totally inappropriate from a human point of view.

Any mother
who would find herself in similar circumstances would have
many questions and doubts,
perhaps even rebellion against the will of God –
so incomprehensible and so difficult to accept.
In every situation
Mary
realized the will of God
with full inner peace,
because she accepted everything with childlike trust.

THE ACCEPTANCE OF EXILE

Shortly after the Son of God was born into the world, the Holy Family had to flee toward Egypt: ". . . behold, the angel of the Lord appeared to Joseph in a dream and said, 'Rise, take the child and his mother, flee to Egypt, and stay there until I tell you. Herod is going to search for the child to destroy him.' Joseph rose and took the child and his mother by night and departed for Egypt" (Mt 2:13-14).

To flee in the middle of the night, leaving everything behind except for some hand luggage, would be terrifying for any family!

It is not difficult to imagine how a young married couple would react to receiving, in the middle of the night, the message to flee the country immediately with their child. Could they leave the house they worked so hard to obtain? Could they leave behind the money they saved which at night cannot be withdrawn from the bank? Could they renounce the work that gives them a sense of security? How would they react to the fact that God wanted them to go to an unknown land without any human securities?

Yet Mary accepted with peace Joseph's announcement that they must escape to Egypt, as 'revealed' to him in a dream by the angel.

Would any other woman behave similarly in a similar situation?

> She, whose life was a continuous reading of the signs
> that God gave her, whose eyes were fixed on God
> and who was listening intently to His word,
> immediately perceived in this event a **sign of God,**
> to which she submitted herself
> totally, without hesitating.
> > It was not important for her that she had to leave everything
> > today
> > or tomorrow,
> > because she put her hope in God
> > and not in what she had to leave behind.

THE DIFFICULTY OF ACCEPTING THE 'ORDINARY' ASPECT OF JESUS

Mary knew that the child who was conceived in her womb by the power of the Holy Spirit would be called the Son of the Most High: ". . . he will rule over the house of Jacob forever, and of his kingdom there will be no end" (Lk 1:33). The Most Blessed

Virgin "had grown up in the midst of these expectations of her people," as John Paul II says.[31]

> However, since the moment of birth,
> the Child seemed to be so ordinary and commonly normal!
> The divine traits were not noticeable in Him.
> He was behaving just like other children.

Since His birth, Mary lived in intimacy with the mystery of the divine/human nature of Jesus and with the mystery of His person being the Son of God, entirely through faith. "If though, from the moment of the Annunciation, the Son – whom only the Father knows completely, as the one who begets him in the eternal 'today' (cf. Ps 2:7) – was revealed to Mary, she, his Mother, is in contact with the truth about her Son only in faith and through faith!"[32]

> How difficult this trial,
> which was prolonged for many years, could have been for her –
> The Son of the Most High was slowly and gradually learning everything,
> just like any other man.
> Mary "continues to *believe day after day*
> amidst all the trials and the adversities of Jesus' infancy . . . ."[33]
> It is true that certain events seemed to confirm
> His divine nature.
> But understanding them properly also demanded faith,
> because their meaning was concealed.
> God did not spare Mary from trials, and in difficult situations
> He did not fully explain everything to her.

---

[31] *RMat* 15.
[32] *RMat* 17.
[33] Ibid.

It can be supposed that she was a witness
of the childlike weakness and helplessness of the Son of God —
whom she wrapped in diapers,
who, without doubt, cried when He was hungry,
who most certainly fell over when making His first steps
and who uttered His first word with difficulty. . . .

Jesus, who grew before Mary's eyes externally appeared as if **only human**. His growth was not accompanied by extraordinary phenomena. Seeing God in her Son, whose humanity made Him completely similar to other children, must have been linked with 'a particular heaviness of heart' and a dark 'night of faith'.[34] In this way, Mary "living side by side with her Son under the same roof, . . . 'advanced in her pilgrimage of faith,'. . ."[35]

THE MYSTERY OF MARY'S GREATNESS

When the little boy Jesus was lost during the pilgrimage to Jerusalem, Mary did not know how long He had been away from her. However, she maintained an unwavering childlike faith and trust when she and Joseph searched for Him. Even afterwards, when she found Him, she listened: "Why were you looking for me?" (Lk 2:49). The Gospel says that "they did not understand what he said to them" (Lk 2:50), and so, she was once again faced with the mystery. Nevertheless, with childlike trust before God

she ponders it in her heart —
in her heart of an evangelical child,
who boundlessly trusts,

---

[34] Cf. RMat 17.
[35] RMat 17.

who does not demand unnecessary explanations
nor desires any argument.

During the public life of Jesus, Mary "*lived in intimacy with the mystery of her Son,* and went forward in her 'pilgrimage of faith,'..."[36] Christ Himself speaks about her life of faith when one of the women among the crowd who was listening to Him exclaimed, "Blessed is the womb that carried you and the breasts at which you nursed" (Lk 11:27). But He said: "Rather, blessed are those who hear the word of God and observe it" (Lk 11:28). Jesus does not contradict the affirming declaration of this unknown woman, but explains that **what constitutes true greatness is the spiritual contact with God,** which reached its fullest dimension in Mary.

Another affirming statement of Jesus carries the same eloquent message which can be referred to Mary: "[For] whoever does the will of God is my brother and sister and mother" (Mk 3:35).

Through attentive listening to the Word of God and its fulfillment
we can be converted into brothers and sisters of Jesus
and imitate the attitude of the Mother of God.

IN HUMILITY AND HIDDENNESS

During the messianic public ministry of Jesus, Mary remains hidden.
Why does she, who is the most open,
who accepts every word of the Son of God
and fully lives by it,

---

[36] Ibid.

not listen directly to His teachings?
Even if this will remain a mystery,
one can nevertheless perceive in this
that God encourages a hidden life.

For us, Mary's attitude is an eloquent testimony of how important it is to imitate Jesus in His humility and in His remaining unnoticed.

For someone who gains recognition by attaining great things, it is difficult to grow in spiritual poverty. And without this growth, it is impossible to fully imitate Christ.

Thus, when it is not necessary that you fulfill something great in the eyes of others, you should want to remain unnoticed and forgotten.

It is not always possible to literally imitate Mary's hidden life. If God wants you to achieve great things visibly, you cannot deny it of yourself. More importantly, **you yourself** must not seek some privilege or that which could make you 'great' in the eyes of the world.

God calls many persons
to imitate the hidden life of Mary.
Perhaps He is also calling you
    to this kind of union with her,
    so that you also
    may slowly disappear,
    and that with joy you may give up your place to others,
    in such a way that nobody may ask about you. . .

AT THE FOOT OF THE CROSS – HEROISM OF OBEDIENCE IN FAITH

The culminating point of Mary's trials of faith was her presence at the foot of the Cross. It was there that she witnessed how her Son "spurned and avoided by men,/ a man of suffering" (Is 53:3), was agonizing on the Cross. She, who believed against all hope, manifested the heroism of obedience in faith.

In fact, Mary never heard that God could be weak, helpless, and subjected to suffering. She had been educated in a monotheistic culture, which taught that God was an omnipotent Creator. On Golgotha, however, the **Son of God** hung helplessly on the Cross and before her eyes, **dying** in unimaginable and unspeakable torture! His death was evident, and there was not a single doubt about it.

> None of this made the faith of Mary waver.
> She was the only one
> who **participated with faith**
> in the miracle
> of the redemption of the world,
> which was taking place on the Cross.

"How great, how heroic then is the *obedience of faith* shown by Mary in the face of God's 'unsearchable judgments'! How completely she 'abandons herself to God' without reserve, 'offering the full assent of the intellect and the will' to Him whose 'ways are inscrutable' (cf. Rom 11:33)!"[37]

---

[37] *RMat* 18.

Standing at the foot of the Cross, Mary trusts
that in these moments the greatest good is being realized –
Jesus, of His own will, freely chooses the Cross,
in order to fulfill the will of the Father.
And so, she adores the Cross with the simplicity of a child,
without analyzing the situation
in which God has placed her.
She does not consider the situation as a desperate or hopeless one,
because her Son, precisely in this manner,
fulfills voluntarily the will of the Father.
What He does, then, is without doubt **the greatest good**.

> Someone who ponders everything only in the light of
> human logic
> will never fully understand the mystery of suffering
> and of the Cross.
> In the face of this mystery
> the attitude of **childlike trust** is essential.

Only when you adopt such an attitude before God
will you become immune to the influence of Satan –
because he, in his temptations, exploits
the way of thinking which is based only
on human reasoning.
Only then will you stop analyzing so much.
God obviously wants
you to be guided by reason –
but by a reason that is illuminated by faith,
which will allow you to discover His will
and fulfill it,
even when His will for you is very difficult to accept.

THE SUFFERING AND CROSSES OF MARY AFTER THE RESURRECTION

Mary advanced in the "pilgrimage of faith" to the very end of her earthly life. After the Resurrection of Christ, she was not kept from new trials and extraordinarily difficult experiences.

After the descent of the Holy Spirit, she experienced, along with the emerging church, the tragedy of the first Christians.

As the Mother of *all* people
she witnessed with unspeakable pain
how some of her children
were torturing and killing her other children.
St. Stephen, who was stoned to death, was her son,
but those who stoned him were her children too.
She was embracing everybody with her maternal love.
God did not keep her from suffering nor from bearing crosses
because she was docile to Him in everything
and wanted to fulfill the mission that her Son entrusted to her
of being the Mother of the Church.

MARY TEACHES US IN THE "PILGRIMAGE OF FAITH"

By preceding us in the "pilgrimage of faith," with the attitude of childlike trust in God, Mary became the perfect instrument of the Holy Spirit. She submitted herself fully to His action and fulfilled everything which He expected from her.

Mary teaches us how to abandon ourselves to God in the experiences which we do not understand and whose meaning we will come to know only, perhaps, in the life to come.

God expects that during the trials of faith
you will want
to acknowledge with humility His inscrutable designs
and you will accept the fact
that you will not understand much of His divine resolutions,
just like her.

The self-abandonment to God may be frequently linked to the loss of all human supports. You will then enter into an ever-increasingly authentic entrustment to God, which will affect all spheres of your life.

OUR UNION WITH THE CRUCIFIED CHRIST

Contemplating the lives of saints, it can be said that from a certain moment, their lives become a chain of ever more difficult experiences and intensifying trials of faith, until finally the dramatic moment of crucifixion arrives. Certainly, many saints then repeat the cry of the Crucified Christ: "My God, my God, why have you forsaken me?" (Mt 27:46).

The perspective of such a path to sanctity may terrify you.
If you have known to some degree and extent your weakness,
you know that by your own strength
you are unable to overcome this trial.
But in fact, **you will not be alone.**
She, who was at the foot of the Cross,

the one who stood at the foot of the Cross of Christ,
will also be with you.

When, at the moment of death,
you are confronted with the greatest trial,
God, through Mary
will surely want to show you His love in a special way.

The desired aim of your way to sanctity
should be your union with the Crucified Christ
and to die in union with Him.
If you do not aspire for this aim in your life
you can despise it.
In fact, you live in order
to enter a new life
after going through many trials
and finally through death.

The way that leads to this aim
is your boundless abandonment to God,
through self-entrustment to Him
like Mary's.

CHAPTER 12

HE REGARDED THE HUMILITY OF HIS "SLAVE"

S t. Paul writes: "But when the fullness of time had come, God sent his Son, born of a woman, born under the law, to ransom those under the law, so that we might receive adoption. As proof that you are children, God sent the spirit of his Son into our hearts, crying out, 'Abba, Father!' So you are no longer a slave but a child, and if a child then also an heir, through God" (Gal 4:4-7).

We receive divine filial adoption by virtue of Christ's sacrifice. As children of God, we become heirs to everything that pertains to our Father.

What a marvelous and awesome perspective is our vocation!

Even with having only a superficial awareness about the extraordinary content of these words, they instill wonder in us and oblige us to make a response.

THE RESPONSE OF MARY

How could we cooperate in the best way with the grace of being children of God? Let us contemplate the one who responded most fully to this grace.

What is the attitude that Mary adopts before the vocation that has been revealed to her? Let us listen anew to her response to the angel: "Behold, I am the handmaid of the Lord. May it be done to me according to your word" (Lk 1:38). In the original Greek, the term *dule* is used. This term generally means a slave, which means a person who can be treated as an object without subjectivity or any rights, and for whom the will of the Lord is completely obligatory. Mary says to God: **I want to be your slave.**

> But St. Paul wrote: "So you are no longer a slave but a child" (Gal 4:7).
> How can this be reconciled with the response of Mary? –
> Mary's declaration is not that of a slave,
> but a child
> who trustfully abandons herself to her Father.
> Being in the presence of the infinite love of God
> that is revealed to her
> and offered this marvelous vocation,
> Mary places her entire life in
> God's hands.

Here, God's generosity meets the most proper human response, which is as a declaration to God the Father:

You, Father, Who give Yourself to me in Your Son
accept my boundless abandonment to You.
Do with me everything that You will.
I entrust myself to You,
and I entrust to You my will
because I believe that Your will is an expression of
unfathomable love.
I want You to accomplish in me
everything to which You are calling me.

THE ONE WHO WANTED TO BE THE SLAVE OF THE LORD

The Blessed Virgin Mary calls herself a slave. She surrenders her freedom to God, and she does not want to have any rights of her own before Him. She expresses in this way her spiritual poverty: before your infinite grandeur, O Lord, I am an 'earthen vessel' (cf. 2 Cor 4:7). And Mary remains profoundly convinced that she is an 'earthen vessel', although she receives the greatest graces which are impossible for us to imagine.

In response to the grace of special election,

she wants to be the last, and she wants to disappear.
She is precisely the first,
because she is the slave of the Lord
and because in her own eyes she is the last.

Mary's attitude of spiritual poverty is not only visible during the Annunciation but also in the other events that the Gospel shows us. When the Son of God comes into the world in inhumane conditions, she accepts everything in total submission.

> She submits herself to the will of God in every situation,
> because being the slave of the Lord
> she does not believe in herself as having rights.

TO REIGN MEANS TO SERVE

God exalted Mary above all creatures and called her to be the Queen of heaven and of earth.

This Queen reigns by serving.

Mary does not seek herself in anything. She serves with her whole life even if the Mother of the Son of God is called to be the Queen of all creatures.

We can ask, why did God elevate Mary to such a great dignity?

> "For he has looked upon his handmaid's lowliness"(Lk 1:48).
> God exalts the humble.

In the meditation of John Paul II before the "Angelus" (23 August 1981) he used the expression: "to reign means to serve." The most perfect image of this affirmation is the life of the Son of God, and among all creatures is the example of Mary's life.

> Mary reigns
> by her conscious election to be the slave of the Lord.
> She has only one desire –
> to fulfill the will of Him who is everything for her.

With her attitude, she repeats continuously her 'fiat' to God;
she accepts any manifestation of the will of God
as the most precious gift.
This is how she passes through life.
She is the first among all creatures.

In Nazareth, everyone thought her to be an ordinary woman and mother. She had no important social standing, being a carpenter's wife. The Mother of God is unnoticeable among the crowd of ordinary and common people. She does not desire anything for herself. With her whole attitude, she affirms:

> I am the slave of the Lord,
> I deserve nothing,
> I only hunger for that which comes from the will of God.

Mary's reign is expressed only in constant service.
She wants to be unnoticed; she wants to disappear –
so that people may direct their attention to the One
who alone is the first and the most important.

SHE NEVER CONCEALED GOD

During the period of Christ's public life, Mary continues living her 'fiat', and she remains totally in the shadow of her Son. She lives a hidden life so as not to conceal Jesus. She is even discreet when she participates in the suffering of her Son. When she is standing at the foot of the Cross, she fully unites herself with Him.

This extraordinary participation of Mary in the suffering of her Son unites her uniquely in the work realized by Jesus, to whom she entrusts herself undividedly for the service of the mystery of redemption. Some saints, among others St. Maximilian, have given the one whose only desire is to be the slave of the Lord, the title Co-Redemptrix.

After Jesus' Ascension into heaven, Mary serves the beginning of the emerging Church. Mary accompanies the Church in her most important events. She is present with the Church during the descent of the Holy Spirit. Nevertheless, she remains in the shadow of the Apostles, the Church's hierarchy constituted by Christ. And they respect her singular desire to remain hidden.

By this attitude, she always points to Christ, the only Redeemer.

YOU MUST DESIRE TO REMAIN HIDDEN AND UNNOTICED

There should be in each one of us the desire of Mary – that of remaining hidden and unnoticed.

If you want to imitate her
your ordinary day to day life should be one of service –
depending on your vocation,
on the work that you do, and
on the conditions of the environment in which you live.

Fix your attention on Mary and try to tell God with greater frequency:

Oh my Beloved,
do with me everything that You may want to do

as if I were an object without any rights or freedom.
You make me free and You recognize me as Your son,
and I in response to Your love
want to be Your slave.
Grant me the grace to be so,
since you know me well, Lord;
otherwise, I will not benefit from the freedom that You bestow
upon me,
whether that of a son or of a child.
You know that otherwise I would waste everything.

TO BE DISPOSED TO TURN OVER YOUR FUNCTIONS TO OTHERS

When you perform an important function in professional or social life, you should try, as much as possible, to 'disappear' like Mary.

You must serve in a way that another person may occupy your place at any moment.

Above all, like Mary, you must not conceal God with your person. And this will only be possible when you become poor in spirit and you want to be the servant-slave of Christ. When speaking with Him, you may repeat often: *Lord, I want to fulfill the function that You have bestowed upon me in the best possible way, but if it would be Your will that another person would fulfill it, then let it be.*

Whatever work you carry out, you should always be ready to relinquish it to others, in conformity to the will of God. Because none of us are immortal and we can die at any time, our service can also come to an end at any moment. Therefore, it is important to edify the authority of others, so that God may be served by them, so that they may assume the functions that we may have complied with up to this hour.

Without such an attitude, it is difficult to imagine the growth of interior life.

Try to live the present moment as if your life would end soon, without anxiety, of course, because everything is in God's hands.

This attitude is an expression of humbling yourself before God
that you may recognize that you are an 'earthen vessel'
that, by itself, is very fragile and incapable of anything.
How could such an object be irreplaceable?
Can God not be served by another 'vessel'?

THE SLAVERY OF ATTACHMENT TO OUR POSITIONS

Excessive attachment to one's job functions is a significant obstacle in striving for sanctity. If ever you do your job with attachment to it and without being disposed to renounce it in favor of others, your sanctification may be made impossible. This attachment to the position that you have is a form of slavery.

Do not yearn to be irreplaceable –
recognize that you are an 'earthen vessel'.
The fact of standing in the truth before God in this way
will set you free –
then God will become for you the first and the most important.
You will always desire to showcase Him,

146

and you will understand that it is not the 'earthen vessel' that is important –
but only He who is served by it.

The fact that God may act through you today does not mean that tomorrow He will not choose another. Could it be that it is precisely your attachment to the function that you perform which is hindering God to act freely?

Or maybe, that you would want 'to manipulate' very discreetly the person to whom you may have handed over your responsibilities? This would be proof that you do not want to be a slave of Christ, or to imitate Mary. And this would be proof that you consider yourself to be a 'golden vessel' which others cannot do without.

The poor in spirit, the one who acknowledges the truth about oneself, is free because the truth liberates. Such a person may not be afraid of dying and of leaving some unfinished important work of one's life. He recognizes his condition as an 'earthen vessel' and does not believe himself to be irreplaceable.

> You must want to fulfill your function,
> if it is God's will,
> but at the same time
> you must be disposed to renounce it without hesitation
> at the same instant God may ask for it.
> This applies even to the function and obligations of parents.

In educating the children, the parents should, above all, try to show God to them. It is obvious that parents have to care for their children. However, in a given moment, when the children may begin to go their own way, the parents should 'disappear' up to a certain degree, so that the children may find more support in God and may begin to look for everything in Him.

DO NOT ASK WHY

If you want to be the servant of Christ, it is possible that He may treat you in different ways:

Sometimes you will receive 'easy' graces,
and at other times 'difficult' ones.

The Lord does not have to explain to His subject why He gives him 'candies' or nourishes him with 'bitterness'.

A servant of *Him*
who is Love,
will never ask *why?*
Mary did not ask this question,
neither during the Annunciation,
nor at the foot of the Cross of her Son.

She was always the slave of God, and this concept has a profound meaning. Whereas nowadays a servant is frequently considered no less important than his lord, it was different during the time of Christ.

We come to know this in the following words that He directed to His Apostles: "I no longer call you slaves, because a slave does not know what his master is doing. I have called you friends, because I have told you everything I have heard from my Father" (Jn 15:15).

This means that the servant did not know what his master was doing and it was demanded from him that he would accept his not knowing – he was converted into a kind of servant-slave.

Mary was a servant precisely in this sense –
accepting not to know.
She only asked that
which was indispensable for the realization of the intention of
the Lord,
in order to realize fully His will.

She was like the evangelical child who trusted fully in the Father and looked at the world with His eyes even if she did not understand everything that happened in her life.

It is necessary that we imitate Mary precisely in her total humiliation before God, in the attitude of a slave. She adopts this attitude because she knows that God is Love, that **her everything is an entrustment into Love.**

If you believe
that in **everything** that God does
there is an expression of His love,
you may not expect special explanations.
You may not analyze
why sometimes you were particularly honored
and at other times – divested of everything.

This attitude will permit you to accept *your own way toward God,* since there are varied ways through which we journey toward Him and frequently these ways are incomprehensible for us.

"How inscrutable are his judgments and how unsearchable his ways!" (Rom 11:33).

But how is this so in my life?
In spite of my efforts, why is it that I continually fall into some vice?
Or, why do I make good resolutions and fall again?
How can it be that I accuse myself contritely in the Sacrament of Reconciliation and sin again with persistence?

If you adopt the attitude of a servant before God, you will easily understand the meaning of this way. Then you will say to yourself: *Without doubt, I am so proud that I have to recognize my evil through sinning. He, in fact, does not wish that I fall and this may wound Him. Nevertheless, He permits it so that I may journey toward my conversion at the expense of His suffering.*

HE HAS LOOKED ON HER HUMILITY

The fragments in the Gospel that speak about Mary present her to us as poor in spirit. The words in the "Magnificat" say that God "has looked upon his handmaid's lowliness" (Lk 1:48).[38]

Mary, standing before God in the truth, recognizes her "lowliness," her being very poor.

To put oneself in the truth
is to recognize
that without the support of God in us, we could be capable
of committing every possible sin.

---

[38] The corresponding Hebraic expression for "lowliness" means "to show mercy by reason of humility." W. Baver, *Griechisch-deutsches Wörterbuch zu Schriften des Neven Testaments und die übrigen urchristlichen Literatur* (Berlin - New York: Kolum, 1988), 588.

Mary was free from every evil not only by the grace of God but also by her cooperation with grace. **Her cooperation consisted, above all, in remaining humble.** Mary was free from original sin and from internal temptations but not from external temptations. Even Jesus himself was tempted. So just as Adam and Eve sinned, Mary also could have sinned – since in fact she was fully free.

Where is the mystery of this marvelous phenomenon hidden, the most marvelous thing that may have occurred any time on earth to such a creature? Certainly it is not only in the grace of God, but also in the response to this grace.

We can think that Mary, perfectly humble,
recognized that she was capable of committing
all possible sins.
Someone who is truly humble never believes
that there are any sins that, with all certainty, one could not commit.
God saw the depth of her humility:
the abyss of her misery on one side
and the abyss of her trust on the other side.
For this, ". . . he has looked upon his handmaid's lowliness."
He preserved her from any sin
and filled her with Himself.
The Mother of the Son of God became a vessel
which God filled,
but such a vessel recognized continually her fragility.
She knew that the treasure of such a gift is God,
whom we carry in "earthen vessels" (2 Cor 4:7).
God filled Mary totally,
since she, remaining in the truth,
continually called on Him.

WITH OUR EYES FIXED ON MARY

We observe that Mary submits herself in everything to the will and to the action of God. She, who always says "yes" to her Lord, the one who calls herself a slave of the Lord, fulfills the will of God in a perfect way. She is like a grain that always submits to some process in accord with the plans of the Creator.

And so it also has to be your attitude in everything
that God has planned for you.
You should be like a grain –
so submissive and absolutely obedient to His will
that you may die and grow exactly like He wants.
Your will should be submitted totally to the Creator.
You will want to die to yourself
to the extent that you will want
to be like her, the 'slave' of the Lord.
It is only then that the process of your dying
and the growth of new life – God's life in you –
will be realized in the optimal way.

And then you will be an instrument
through which God can be served
for the realization of His plans
in your neighborhood
in your city
in your country
in the whole world.
Such is the plan of God for each one of us.

CHAPTER 13

FILIAL SELF-ENTRUSTING TO MARY

W hen on the way to sanctity we pass through the stage of the desert, very gloomy thoughts regarding our future often torment us. The present may also trouble us when we do not want to accept the situation which has arisen and we begin to rebel.

To pass through these experiences and the torments of a spiritual desert can be very difficult, since they are frequently the result of being misunderstood by those around us and of rejection or of unjust accusations.

THE VOCATION OF THE APOSTLES ON THE WAY OF THE CROSS

St. John the Evangelist was faced with the prospect of such experiences on the day of Christ's death. Standing at the foot of the Cross he was hearing the hostile jeers and mockeries all the while his beloved Teacher was dying. Thus, his future could have appeared to him as terrifying. St. John, whose faith was not yet fully formed, could have feared that as a disciple of the One Condemned, he would **also** be accused, submitted to repression, persecuted and perhaps even crucified.

In contemplating the way through which the Apostles were led, we discover that at the moment of the arrest and crucifixion of Christ, they felt and experienced that everything was crumbling and the 'ground was giving way under their feet'. It could have appeared to them that what they considered as the supreme value,

> their plans and dreams,
> the whole reality of their lives up to this moment –
> everything was falling down.

The day of Christ's death for them was the day of 'total defeat'.

Jesus, before his death, prepared the Apostles to accept the truth that He Himself, as well as His disciples, would have to go through the way of the Cross. However, despite being assured that they would go through this way, and despite their verbal declarations, they betrayed Him at the moment of the trial.

At that time, they were not yet accepting His call, although later, all, except Judas, were fully united with the Crucified One.

OUR RESISTANCE AND REBELLIONS

We also continuously defend ourselves from following the way of the Cross.

We know, however, that we should imitate Christ, even if slightly difficult situations arise or if we lose something. Our immediate reactions are resistance and protest.

Our whole nature protests.
We are practically ready and disposed to stop believing in God,
who does not satisfy our expectations and our egoism.

In some instances, we demonstrate our rebellions,
and at other times they are hidden in us.

One form of rebellion is our submission to temptations and, as a consequence, our consent to sin.

Rebellion is also expressed in our hopelessness in our attitude
to the future.
Nothing interests us anymore,
we think that in the end we have to lose everything
which up to now has been the source of our joy.
The perspective of the future appears to us to be ever darker,
less interesting and depressing.

In the process of purifications, God will be freeing you
from the illusions and from the idols that, before, you
were adoring.
You can have, therefore, the impression
that you are more and more restricted,
more and more weak
and even helpless,
as if an invisible rope is tightening around

your neck.

At that point you may be irritated and angry.

But Jesus very clearly says that everyone who would follow Him must take up the cross of everyday life and carry it until the moment arrives that one has to die on it – just like Him.

And with this a very strong rebellion can appear, so strong that it can terrify you.

WHEN OUR WEAKNESS TERRIFIES US

In certain stages of interior life, you will indeed discover something terrifying in yourself. You will be convinced that it would be pure folly to go the way of the Cross. You will know when the experiences of the desert are intensified; as soon as you enter into an increasing degree of darkness – everything begins to rebel in you.

Then you will question yourself:

How can I go this way?

In every temptation, in every trial of faith

I am convinced of my weakness;

how can I follow the way of Jesus?

Do not be afraid – there is also an opportunity for the weak and for those who have not yet totally believed. The words of Christ's testament pronounced from the Cross to Mary and St. John are a sign of hope for everybody:

"Woman, behold, your son . . .

Behold, your mother" (Jn 19:26-27).

While dying on the Cross, the Savior **confides** His mother to John, and, at the same time, **entrusts** John and everyone for whom He was dying, to her who abandoned herself totally to God.[39]

> Therefore, do not be terrified by your own weakness.
> You yourself, with your own efforts, will never choose the way of the Cross.
> But in fact, the words of Christ's testament
> are a **special gift** for you.
> You also are a child of the Mother of God —
> you have a particular right to these words.
> Therefore, why are you afraid?
> Why do you want to carry your cross alone?
> In fact, this is the precise cause of your torment!
> In your stubbornness and pride, you want to carry your cross by yourself.
> But, in fact, you will not carry it alone.
>
> Christ wants
> you to ask Him for help from His mother.

THE CALL TO COMMUNION OF LIFE WITH MARY

> Jesus entrusts John
> and each one of us
> to His mother.
> What does it signify?

John Paul II writes: "Entrusting himself to Mary in a filial manner, the Christian, like the Apostle John, 'welcomes' the

---

[39] Cf. RMat 45.

Mother of Christ 'into his own home'[130] and brings her into everything that makes up his inner life, that is to say into his human and Christian 'I' . . . ."[40]

> With His testament from the Cross, Jesus calls
> each one of us
> to build a communion of life with Mary.
> The Savior wills
> that we may introduce His mother
> into our interior life, so that she can form us.

The words he "took her into his home" (Jn 19:27) signify not only that St. John took Mary in his own house and took care of her; they also signify a completely new form of interpersonal relationship – **a communion of life** between St. John and the Mother of God.

The entrusting of Mary as a mother to St. John constitutes a new "intimate relationship of a child with its mother."[41]

The entrusting of oneself to Mary leads to a special relationship with her. Through Christ's death, God pours His unfathomable love, fatherly and motherly love, over the world. He wants it to reach the very depths of our hearts **through the heart of Mary.**

---

[40] See endnote 130 in *Rmat* p. 79 that states: "Clearly, in the Greek text the expression '*eis tà ídia*' goes beyond the mere acceptance of Mary by the disciple in the sense of material lodging and hospitality in his house; it indicates rather a *communion of life* established between the two as a result of the words of the dying Christ: cf. Saint Augustine, *In Ioan. Evang. tract.* 119, 3: CCL 36, 659: 'He took her to himself, not into his own property, for he possessed nothing of his own, but among his own duties, which he attended to with dedication.'"
[41] *RMat* 45.

This great grace requires a response.
The response that God expects
is your entrustment to Mary,
which is expressed
in **living this special relationship with her.**

THE DIFFERENCE BETWEEN 'ENTRUSTING MARY TO JOHN' AND 'ENTRUSTING JOHN TO MARY'

There is a big difference between these two 'entrustings'. John Paul II writes: "The Redeemer entrusts Mary to John because he entrusts John to Mary."[42]

Christ "entrusts" Mary to John,
so that he may take care of her.
On the other hand he "entrusts" John to Mary,
in the same way God
entrusts
a child
to its mother.

This act gives birth to her child.
Mary lives in a singular union with him
and loves him as if he were her only child.
For this, the child
with unwavering trust
can entrust himself in total abandonment of himself to her.

In entrusting himself to Mary, John introduces her into his interior life in order to share with her everything that constitutes his inner 'I'.

---

[42] *RMat* 45.

As the Pope says: "Such entrusting is *the response* to a person's love, and in particular *to the love of a mother*."[43]

THE INTIMATE RELATIONSHIP WITH THE MOTHER

From then on, John will resolve all important matters
with the Mother of God,
asking her to intervene in all of his experiences –
even the most personal ones.
He wants her to lead him
like a mother leads her child.
You also begin
to build your interior relationship with Mary –
just like that of a little child
with its mother who loves it.
Introduce her
into the most intimate dimension and realms of your life.
Try to maintain always a spiritually childlike attitude.
You must want to be weak like a child,
whose own possibilities are almost useless.

FACING TRIALS AND DIFFICULT EXPERIENCES

Adopting this attitude simplifies to a large extent the passage through diverse trials and difficult experiences. To someone who abandons himself to Mary, it will be easier for him to have the attitude of a child of God; the attitude of a child who, in believing that it is loved and fully accepted, guards in every

RMat 45.

situation the dignity which is proper to him. Then, being rejected by other people, for example, is no longer so painful.

If God does not reject me,
then being rejected by other people is only
to purify me
of excessive attachments,
of depending on people too much,
and of trying to gain for myself a good opinion in the eyes of the
world.

Anyone whose attitude is that of a child of God is being led in some manner by Mary, and is not overtaken

> by accusations,
> by bad opinion,
> by being misunderstood,
> by rejection.

He will want to be recognized by others only if it is the will of God. The filial self-abandonment to Mary frees us from that which greatly restricts us: from the unnecessary and inappropriate compromise with the world.

When someone is entrusted to Mary,
desiring that she may form one's interior life,
sanctification becomes the aim of one's life;
that is to say, being permeated by Christ in such a way
that one's 'self' may disappear all the more
so that Christ may begin to live in him.

This is realized normally in the context of being rejected by other people. Being scorned and misunderstood becomes an ordinary occurrence on our way toward sanctity.

A child of God being led by Mary is certain that God loves him in spite of the abyss of one's evil. He believes that the abyss of God's Love exceeds in an infinite way even the deepest abyss of human nothingness and of sin.

In fulfilling the will of God, he is not afraid whether or not he will be understood and accepted. If Christ, who leads him, wants him to remain in the limelight and realize an apostolate with his word, he will accomplish it believing that Christ Himself will speak through him. Christ will use him to fulfill the will of God, because everything is possible through Him. And when he may be humiliated, he will accept it with dignity, because not a single humiliation will shake his faith in the fact that he is loved.

This attitude can appear in our life thanks to "this filial entrusting to the Mother of Christ." [44]

The filial abandonment to Mary is an opportunity for each one of us to enter into a very personal and intimate contact with our spiritual mother, so that we will permit her[45] to participate in the fullest way in the formation of our interior life.

Christ wants you to introduce Mary into your whole life,
into your most intimate interior experiences.
He wants you to imitate her in the best possible way.

Then you will become strong with the power of her Son.

---

[44] RMat 45.
[45] LG 62.

TO IMITATE MARY IN EVERYTHING

The intimate contact with his mother causes the son, by observing her, and without taking notice, to begin to look at everything through her eyes. A little child imitates its mother consciously or unconsciously since it shares with her everything which it experiences. She also participates in its interior experiences.

This is precisely what must happen in the case of a child of God. A child, in entrusting itself filially to its spiritual Mother, begins to share with her its whole life, **forming a communion of persons.**[46] The child has its eyes fixed intently on her, and without even knowing when, tries to imitate her **fully:**

in her way of looking at the world,
in her way of thinking,
in her values,
in her prayer and in her life.
By imitating Mary,
we unite ourselves with Christ
and it is no longer ourselves who live but Him who
lives in us (cf. Gal 2:20).

TO LET ONE'S SELF BE FORMED BY HER

The child, in responding to the love of its Mother and in abandoning itself to her, permits her to form its interior life like that of hers.

---

[46] Entering in communion with Mary must be understood as a full imitation of her attitude before God.

John received this inexpressible grace in the moment when everything was at its darkest and when everything seemed to be falling apart. For him, dying was a sign of something new – some kind of a new world, which would come after the consummation of the mystery of the Cross.

> If someday everything for you is falling apart,
> it can mean
> that you must build an even more profound communion of life
> with Mary, your spiritual Mother.
>> A child of God who goes out to meet his Mother,
>> and without fear permits her to form him,
>> begins to live in another way.
>> His life is transformed,
>> even though he does not necessarily know why.

Obviously this will be a process; generally nothing is realized in our interior life instantaneously, with the wave of a magic wand. Its growth requires time and effort. Moreover, we frequently realize it in an imperceptible way.

And this – process of formation of our filial relationship with Mary – does not transpire without difficulties, because a person who is spiritually old wants to decide his destiny by himself alone.

> Perhaps too often you do not trust in Mary
> because you continually trust in yourself.
> Perhaps you are rebelling,
> and you do not want to accept the gifts
> that God bestows on you through the hands of Mary.
> But, in fact, only when you are small,

helpless
and boundlessly trustful in God,
will you be bestowed with true power.

A child of God who is helpless and trusting boundlessly in His mercy has the power of the Creator Himself at his disposal.

Nothing is impossible
for someone who remains before God with a spiritually
childlike attitude.
The building of communion of life with Mary will become
your
way to sanctification.
This is an extraordinary opportunity for you.

Of course, if you prefer, you can try to carry your cross by yourself and imitate Christ on your own. This is also possible. But, if you are given the grace of understanding who Mary is to you, then you must take advantage of this gift.

Your interior dialogue with Mary will be creating this admirable communion. Thanks to this communion you will be formed in her likeness. And this means that you will begin to live more and more as she lived.

If you entrust yourself to Mary, she will open you most fully to the Holy Spirit, and she will teach you to benefit from His gifts.

This will become your way to the deepest possible life in faith.

CHAPTER 14

IN THE ARMS OF
THE MOTHER

The fulfillment of the will of God in everything is possible only to a person who is in love with Him. Only such a person shows a kind of 'folly' both in what he desires and in what he does. To others, such a person's desires and actions may appear as a kind of 'folly'.

Our spiritual Mother wants to lead us to the love of God that reaches that point of folly. Therefore, complete abandonment to her becomes the way to the most profound love of God.

By the will of her only Son, she is our spiritual Mother and loves us in the same way that she loved her child – Jesus. From the moment of the Incarnation, Mary abandoned herself completely to the disposition of her Son, fulfilling her mission as a mother. All that she did for Him and with Him was connected to salvation and to our spiritual life.

MOTHER AND TEACHER OF OUR LIFE

The Second Vatican Council says that through her maternal commitment with Jesus, Mary cooperated fully with the work of Redemption for the renewal of supernatural life in the life of the souls of men. And so by conceiving, giving birth to, and feeding Christ, and by offering Him in the temple to the Father along with participating in Jesus' suffering on the Cross . . . she became our Mother in the order of grace.[47]

In the realization of her vocation as Mother of Jesus, Mary employed all her physical and spiritual forces. Totally and until the end, she binds herself in the prolongation of this vocation, which is

> her spiritual maternity with respect to us.
> She lives for us,
> takes care of us
> and is completely at our disposal.

From the moment of our conception, Mary is present with each one of us –

> serves us through our earthly mothers
> for whom she intercedes to obtain the necessary graces.

She is closer to us more than our earthly mothers, whose possibilities are limited. The heavenly Mother is continually 'at the disposal' of each of her children; she is disposed to help every time they call upon her.

---

[47] Cf. LG 61.

When you begin to look at your life in the light of faith, you will discover that it was she who watched over you in the night,

> who fed you and took care of you,
> who watched over you in every moment of
> your life.

She cared for you through the doctor who treated you. It was she who showed you love through all the persons who did something good for you.

It was through her intercession that you encountered so much kindness and affection.

Mary is continually with you and takes care of your integral development. In a special way, she takes care of your spiritual growth. **She is Mother and Teacher of your interior life.**

Her deepest desire is that Christ may grow in you in a way that there is no longer any place in your heart for yourself but only for Him and for His will.

The most important element is your openness to the love of God – the attitude of abandonment, simplicity, and the humility of an evangelical child. It is this openness that determines our prayer and bonding with God.

However, in periods when dryness and darkness of faith escalate, our lukewarmness may become greater. Then, contrary to everything we might experience, we should search for ways to incessantly animate our spirit of prayer. When you begin to lose the sense of God's presence, try all the more and with greater intensity to become aware of this presence, through, for example, certain images that illustrate the love of God.

'BEING CARRIED IN THE ARMS OF MARY'

You can, for example, try to see yourself as being carried in the arms of Mary to whom Christ gave us as Mother, saying "'Woman, behold, your son'" (Jn 19:26). From the moment these words were pronounced, Mary has loved all men the way she loved her only Son in His human nature when He lived on earth. Jesus is her son while St. John and every other human being who lives in the world becomes her son.

The love of the Mother is manifested also through various gestures. She shows tenderness to her son, for example, by taking him in her arms. It is a gesture that cuddles her child close to her heart, and, at the same time, it is a gesture which elevates the child. A child who is elevated to the level of the face of the mother feels safe, and is as great as its mother.

Mary, who was given to us as our Mother, carried Christ in her arms. We have the right to think that she 'carries us in her arms', also. When Jesus told His mother: "'Woman, behold, your son'" it was as if He was telling her: My Mother, from this day on you will care for all people and you will 'carry all of them in your arms' as your children in the same way that you carried Me. And the words addressed to John: "'Behold, your mother'" (Jn 19:27) can be interpreted as: John, from today you have the special right to benefit from the privilege of being Mary's child – this privilege consists of being 'carried in the arms of My mother' who is also your Mother.

> When you contemplate an image of Mary,
> you can always remember
> that you are in her arms
> like Jesus was –
> and this is not an exaggeration.

Accepting this truth demands faith to the point of folly. You can only recognize it with the attitude of an evangelical child. Decide for yourself, even if it be by a folly of faith to a small degree, and accept this mystery of God's love! It will become a source of your consolation and joy that will permit you to live with the faith of a child even in the most difficult moments.

'REMAINING IN THE ARMS OF MARY' IN ONE'S INTERIOR LIFE

That Mary 'carries us in her arms' is an objective truth that does not depend on your faith. The words of Christ's testament pronounced on the Cross are, in fact, an objective truth on the maternity of Mary in relation to all men. Her maternity does not depend on our recognition of it nor in our belief in her.

> Independently, whether or not you believe it,
> whether or not you remember it,
> you are 'in the arms of Mary'.

The recognition and acceptance of this truth can become an opportunity to open oneself to God and to His mercy.

It can become an essential element of your spiritual life.

The awareness that Mary 'carries you in her arms' will enable you to remain in God's presence with unfaltering faith in His love. This awareness does not suppose necessarily emotional experiences. Perhaps in some stages of your interior life you may not feel anything at all, but, in spite of it, this awareness will constitute an essential element of your interior life.

Otherwise, if you do not accept this truth
or you rapidly forget it,
you will be sentencing yourself to unnecessary torments,
which is accompanied by the spirit of the attitude of the old man.

The spirit of the old man – contrary to that of the evangelical child – wants to solve problems by itself. And so it exposes itself to the temptations of Satan, it immerses itself in the evil of this world and commits sin.

Consequently, the man condemns himself to suffering.
If he would have the wisdom of the attitude of an evangelical child, he would not have to suffer for his own fault.

A child knows that all his 'grandeur' comes from his mother who raises him on high. And if he forgets it, appropriating this 'grandeur' to himself, he will begin to believe that he is great like her. He would certainly fall rapidly from her arms, which could bring him tragic consequences.

THE PRIVILEGE OF 'REMAINING IN THE ARMS OF MARY' CALLS FOR A COMMITTED RESPONSE

By embracing her children with her special love, The Most Blessed Virgin also 'raises them up on high'. She does this in such a way that very often they do not even realize to whom they should be grateful for this 'elevation'.

However, when, by the will of God, Mary chooses someone as her special instrument, she shows him very clearly how little he is. She shows him that he finds himself exalted only because she 'carries him in her arms'. And so, it is a special grace if you discover the maternal role of Mary in your life.

Why do you receive this grace?
This is a mystery of God's election.
But remember, the grace needs a committed response.
You do not receive a talent in order to bury it in the ground.
You must make use of it – in accordance with the will of God –
for your own sanctification and for the sanctification of others.
Because of this, implore Mary that your whole life
may be permeated by the awareness
that you are 'carried by her in her arms'.

'IN THE ARMS OF MARY' IN THE CONTEXT OF ONE'S EVERYDAY LIFE

This awareness of 'being in the arms of Mary' will be perceived in different forms depending on the stage of spiritual life. It can be fortified by positive emotional sentiments or can be a result only of faith.

Your prayer, in a special way, should be particularly permeated by this great mystery of God's love. The conviction that by the will of God you are 'in the arms of Mary' must accompany you above all when you participate in the Holy Mass and when you go to confession. In this spirit, you can meditate, you can pray with the prayer of the tax collector or with any other form of prayer. By praying for others you can also ask, through her, for openness to this unfathomable divine grace.

The conviction that Mary 'carries you in her arms' must accompany all your actions in your daily life. Whether that with which you occupy yourself is important or insignificant, you are always in her arms.

'In her arms' you work,

you eat,

you drink coffee.

'In her arms' you are falling asleep and you sleep.

Try to begin each day with an act of faith
in the fact that, in His unfathomable love for you, **God wants**
Mary to carry you in the same way she carried her only Son.

'REMAINING IN MARY'S ARMS' EVEN WHEN YOU SIN

Mary does not let you out of her embrace even when you sin, especially if the sin could bring you irreparable damage. Otherwise, sin could become a catastrophe from which you would be unable to turn back. When you believe that you are 'in her arms' it is easier for you to rise from your fall and return to the life of grace. This faith ensures that a sin may not cause an avalanche of more sins.

The arms of the Mother of God are the special place
in which you can rise again from every sin.

'In her arms' you will more easily know your weakness.
You will know that by yourself, you are incapable of imitating Christ.

You must not forget that Mary suffers with great pain the torment that your sin causes Christ. For her, it is excruciatingly painful when you despise His love, when you abuse your own dignity and show contempt to God who loves you extremely and without end.

In spite of this great suffering, she does not let you go from her embrace. If in this moment she would abandon you to your own possibilities – you would perish.

Perhaps it may be difficult for you to believe in this when you do not feel or perceive her presence. God may permit the obscurities of faith and the lack of positive sentiments, so that your faith may grow. He Himself acts through Mary and her hands symbolize the merciful hands of the Father, in which we live as His children and our existence is sustained.

MARY BEFORE HER CRUCIFIED SON

Jesus carried the Cross before the presence of His mother.
She did not try to carry it with Him physically –
she knew that the will of God was otherwise.

Did she not want to help Him at that moment?
Did she not love Him then?
She knew that the best way of helping Christ
was in fulfilling the will of God.
And God wanted the Mother of His Son
to help Him in a way that was
spiritual and not physical.
She fully respected this will of God.

When Jesus was crucified, she did not protect His hands with her own as they were being nailed; neither did she try to remove the nails that had been hammered into His hands and feet. Such behavior would have been completely understandable, because a mother would prefer to suffer herself than to watch the suffering of her son. When Jesus was dying on the Cross, she did nothing that brought consolation to His physical pain and sufferings. She knew that God the Father was allowing and accepting the terrible torment and loneliness of her Son. Because of this, she was accompanying Him in a way full of discretion.

Mary did not help Christ in a visible form, like Simon of Cyrene did for Him. She knew that the will of God was that He would be helped by someone who would be obliged to do it.

By the will of God, Mary remained at a certain distance, although she accompanied Him in everything He endured in the most profound way; when they nailed Him on the Cross, she was spiritually crucified with Him.

MARY'S PRESENCE IN OUR CRUCIFIXION

You can suppose that Mary behaves
      in the same way with us.
When you carry the cross of your purifications,
the cross with everything that God permits
so that you will be converted and may change
– when the old man that exists in you is nailed to the cross –
she is near,
she helps you,
even though you may not be feeling it or seeing it.
Mary acts in this way because she respects the mystery
of God's will.
She knows that you also have to experience to a certain degree the
same situation as that of Jesus:
      the bitterness of loneliness
      being abandoned by those close to you.
When you carry the cross,
she 'carries you in her arms' together with your cross
regardless of whether or not you perceive it.

God will not reveal everything to you because He wants you
to grow in faith. Neither will He reveal to you the truth that the
arms of Mary sustain you, a truth that expresses His
unfathomable love for you. So do not be surprised that she
'carries you in her arms' in a manner most discreet. He does not
make you feel her presence, even when it appears that this
weakens you in the struggle against infidelity and sin.

Believe that when the time comes for you to die, you will be
'in her arms'. She herself will lead you across the frontier of

177

fullness of life. Do not be afraid when at the moment of death you see the abyss of your evil within you – in believing that Mary 'carries you in her arms' you will remain in the arms of divine mercy. Then, more than ever, you will be completely immersed in the mercy of God.

Mary will be holding you in the same way that she held the body of Christ after it had been taken down from the Cross. Death is terrifying, because it is the moment of the final and, probably, greatest darkness.

If, however, you have a childlike attitude and faith in God who loves you in spite of your nothingness, you will not be afraid at the final moment of your life. Do not forget that you are in her hands, even when you least realize it – at times which will be for you a special grace from God – when you would cry out in a way similar to that of Christ: "'My God, my God why have you forsaken me?'"(Mt 27:46).

> She always accompanies you in your suffering,
> and therefore, knows fully the meaning of your suffering.
> Because of this, she expects that you may believe that everything
> that you are confronted with is a grace that God gives you;
> suffering can free you from your various attachments,
> it can destroy your false vision of the world and of God,
> thus bringing you closer to Him.
> > Mary, as Mother of the Church, is the model
> > after which our souls are molded.
> > This is a process that is realized little by little, that lasts
> > a lifetime,
> > and reaches its completion at the moment of death.

If it does not happen that way,
its realization will be continued – in purgatory.
However, God wants
that you may be fully molded here on earth
according to the example of Mary.
He wants you to be sanctified in the midst of the experiences
of life.
If you begin to unite yourself totally to the will of God,
you will be united to the Crucified Christ.

If it is given to you to arrive at this degree of union with Christ in His passion, and for this you die in the midst of great suffering, in loneliness, and in abandonment: remember that Mary will be with you in the way she was with her only Son.

You have the right to have such a relationship with Mary,
like the one which existed between Jesus in His human nature
and her.
You are an adopted child,
by the virtue of Christ's testament on the Cross.

In knowing the love of Mary,
you will know very well that God loves you –
because it is He who shows you His love through her.[48]
God communicates His love to us through the intercession of Mary.
In discovering this unfathomable love
you will want to respond to Him,
and then you can reach full union with Christ.

This is the greatest grace which you can be bestowed with here on earth.

---

[48] Cf. *LG* 62.

About the Author

Slawomir Biela was born in Poland in 1956. He studied at the Warsaw University of Technology, where he earned his doctorate in physics. He also studied at the Papal Faculty of Theology in Warsaw, especially in the field of the Theology of Spirituality.

Since 1977, Slawomir Biela has been cooperating very closely with Rev. Tadeusz Dajczer, Professor of Theology, who is also the founder of the Families of Nazareth Movement. Together, through countless and laborious efforts, they laid the foundation for the spirituality of this worldwide movement.

Consequently, since 1986, Slawomir has been a member of the editorial team responsible for editing various publications pertaining to the spiritual formation of the members of the Movement. Because of their timely issues, these publications have been translated into fourteen languages.

The book *In the Arms of Mary* [1] is the fruit of the author's many years of deep reflections and insights regarding the Christian spiritual life. In it he refers to and explains the various stages of the interior life. For this very reason, the book can serve as a resource for spiritual renewal for both beginners as well as those who are more advanced on the path toward a 'transforming union' with Christ.

---

[1] Published in Great Britain and in the United States as *Praying Self-Abandonment to Divine Love*, cf. Slawomir Biela, *Praying Self-Abandonment to Divine Love* (London: Science Press, 2002).

The book *In the Arms of Mary* presents the same thrust or vein of spirituality as the author's other books such as *God Alone Suffices* and *Behold I Stand at the Door and Knock*. It is worth noting that these books are being published and/or translated in English (Great Britain, USA, the Philippines, Ireland and Canada), Portuguese (Portugal and Brazil), Spanish (Spain, Argentina and Mexico), Dutch, Italian, Catalan, Lithuanian, Bulgarian, German, French, Ukrainian, Loutish, Russian, Hungarian, Czech, Slovenian, Romanian, Albanian, Korean and Vietnamese.

This book presents the same spirituality as the worldwide bestseller *Inquiring Faith*[2] by Rev. Tadeusz Dajczer, Professor of Theology, which has been translated into over 40 languages.

---

[2] In the United States known as *The Gift of Faith*, cf. Father Tadeusz Dajczer, *The Gift of Faith*, 2d ed. (Ventura, CA: In the Arms of Mary Foundation, c.2001).

IN THE ARMS OF MARY
(a.k.a. PRAYING SELF-ABANDONMENT TO DIVINE LOVE)

This book is the fruit of Slawomir Biela's many years of deep reflections and insights regarding the Christian spiritual life. In it he explains and refers to the various stages of one's interior life and offers a pathway to deepening one's prayer. For this very reason, *In the Arms of Mary* can serve as a resource for spiritual renewal both for beginners and those who are more advanced on the path towards a "transforming union with Christ."

GOD ALONE SUFFICES

In this book Slawomir Biela expounds on various ways that an individual can grow in their interior life by letting go of the illusions of this world, and replacing them with total reliance on God. The author guides his reader on a path toward complete surrender of self to the God of love.

BEHOLD I STAND AT THE DOOR AND KNOCK

"Behold I stand at the door and knock. If anyone hears my voice and opens the door, then I will enter his house and dine with him and he with me" (Rev 3:20). This book leads the reader to discover the constant loving and merciful Presence of God. God never leaves His beloved children alone. He is always at the door of our hearts knocking, awaiting our opening of ourselves to Him. Discover the different ways God knocks, why we hesitate to open the door of our heart, and what treasure lies ready for us when we do open the door to our Creator.

OPEN WIDE THE DOOR TO CHRIST

Continuing the themes presented in *Behold, I Stand at the Door and Knock*, Biela helps to convince the reader of the treasure that awaits when we finally open wide the doors to our Creator. He reminds us of the key: spiritual poverty. "Blessed are the poor in spirit, for theirs is the kingdom of heaven" (Mt 5:3). But how to become poor in spirit? That is exactly what this book addresses. A must read for all who desire transforming union with Christ.

Other Books in This Spirituality

THE GIFT OF FAITH, by Father Tadeusz Dajczer

An international bestseller in the field of Christian spirituality, this book about the interior life is a call to abandon oneself to God according to the Gospel edict: "unless you turn and become like children, you will not enter the kingdom of Heaven." With simplicity and clarity, the author manages to draw the reader's attention and awaken the yearning to experience God and to follow a specific path toward sanctity.

IN THE ARMS OF MARY FOUNDATION
P.O. Box 271987
Fort Collins, CO 80527-1987

If *In the Arms of Mary* has helped you to appreciate God's immense love and mercy, then consider donating to **In the Arms of Mary Foundation** to help in the spreading of this spirituality (Communion of life with Christ through Mary) throughout the U.S.A. and the World. Send checks or money orders payable to **In the Arms of Mary Foundation** to the above address.

For more information about the Foundation "In the Arms of Mary" or to obtain additional copies of this book, or other books on this spirituality, please visit our website at www.IntheArmsofMary.org.